Contents

We dedicate this book to all the individuals
who have helped our family throughout the years.

Preface

Sometimes the incidents that threaten our life may strengthen the life in us. Loss and crisis often activate the will to live the way God intended. We can advance and make spiritual progress by facing challenges and obstacles in a spiritual manner.

Earlier on in my marriage, I didn't possess these insights. Upon receiving devastating news about my husband, I questioned God's love for me and my own worthiness. I read and was moved by the words of Minnie Louise Haskins, "Go out into the darkness and put your hand into the Hand of God. That shall be to you better than light and safer than a known way."

And so I searched for spiritual answers. For six of the most difficult years of my life, I kept a journal. I recorded premonitions and instructions that I believed the Lord was delivering to me through prayer, reflection, and dreams that occurred at night. I came to understand, revere, and communicate with God in tender and powerful ways.

Ten years after my husband's death, I found a slip of paper in the bottom of a nightstand drawer. "2004 Family Goals," Dave had written at the top, followed by a short list of aspirations.

Be more kind and generous.
Control temper.
Noise in our house needs to drop a few decimal points.
Improve prayer life.

Find strength in righteousness.

On the other side of this piece of paper, he wrote,

Lessons learned from dying:
It is easier to die, when you are really loved.
Love more and say less.
Live as if you are going to die, and get all things in order....
And love even more.

I have never considered myself a writer and yet felt called to write a book. Why share the most sacred events of my life? The answer that came from the Lord through prayer was clear: "Do you think I gave you these experiences to profit only you? I love all my children. I want all to know and rely on me as you have learned to do." This answer and the words from Dave's "Lessons Learned from Dying," especially about loving, further fueled the desire in me to tell our family's story.

Through mighty prayer and perfect alignment, I was introduced to Kim Douglas at a wellness conference that she was not planning to attend. As destiny would have it, she changed her mind at the last moment and a mutual friend connected us because I had an available spot for her in my hotel room. Through sharing significant life events that had shaped us, we discovered that we held similar values and beliefs about life, love, and God. We became instant friends, and our connection has deepened through the years. We refer to each other as sisters of the heart.

My thoughts about pursuing the idea of writing a book were coming together when God brought everything to a screeching halt. A traumatic health event involving my daughter, Sarah, required all of my attention. Sarah's desire during these difficult days was to show the world what is possible when we choose to partner with God. God preserved her life. We stand as witnesses to His healing power. During her recovery, we both learned that although tangible blessings are miraculous, the greatest miracles are intangible. Although health restored is amazing, hope restored is more miraculous.

When I felt ready to move forward with the book, I reached out to Kim believing God had already opened wide the door for the miraculous fulfillment of such an effort. An author, Kim also served as a professor of writing for twenty-eight years and had previous experience in publishing. We agreed to work together. As my writing coach and editor, she read through hundreds of pages of journal entries and saw possibilities. She inspired Sarah and me to develop our stories and add details that would help the reader better appreciate our experiences. She organized, shaped, and crystalized my words into this very book.

All three of us — Kim, Sarah, and me — feel grateful for each other and for God's divine assistance and guidance every step of the way in creating this book. We reflect on Dave's *lessons from dying* to love even more. We pray that our readers will come to regard their lives as precious gifts, to love even more, and to develop a sacred partnership with the Lord.

Rachel Smartt
Peachtree City, GA

Writing for Transformation

If spirituality is one of the greatest of God's gifts, you are about to receive a powerful present as you read *Modern Day Miracles* by Rachel and Sarah Smartt. Both women, mother and daughter, live their lives by placing their whole faith and confidence in the Lord, not on things that will eventually pass away. They see in everything a message from God. During difficulties, they are not exempt from fear, sadness, and grief. During these times, they are lovingly watchful of one another, trust that God will guide them, and that God's wisdom will become apparent.

When I met Rachel Smartt several years back, I wept for weeks afterwards when I retold her story to others. Her journey needed to be shared. I didn't weep because I felt pity for Rachel, or sorrow. My tears were shed because Rachel's story transformed me. Deeply. Her story demonstrated humility. Someone who possesses humility, to me, is someone who understands from the very depths of their being that it is God, and God alone, that empowers us to traverse through life's challenges and tragedies, and ultimately transforms us in who He wants us to be. Rachel made the decision to walk through a tragedy with God as her most sacred partner. Because of that and the insights gained, we are all blessed to learn from her.

When I met Sarah Smartt, I could see in her the possibilities of our collective future. When children are raised as souls and with intention, they can become radiant and joyful beings. Sarah is such a woman. Sarah, as a young girl and youth, journeyed through their family's crisis and then faced a life-threatening challenge of her own. She was equipped to do so. She had been taught to make the conscious choice to submit to the Will of God, no matter what her emotional or physical condition, because that's what her parents modeled during their struggles and joys. Sarah is a young woman who is transforming our world through her work as an educator. Her students and the students to come will be encouraged, loved, and changed in great ways by her influence.

I treasure my work as a writer and writing coach. After twenty-eight years of teaching writing, I created Transformation Now to support individuals who have a story to share that inspires change. Rachel, Sarah, and I have no doubt that our All-Powerful God connected us. What an honor to use my gifts to serve in the creation of this book. The purpose of life is transformation, to draw ever closer to God, to grow spiritually each and every day. This book will inspire everyone who is fortunate to read it to engage in life's most important work.

Kim Douglas, Director
Transformation Now –
Writing to Transform the World

Foreword

As I started reading *Modern Day Miracles* by Rachel and Sarah Smartt, I jotted down snippets and notes on what I liked most—one liners, lessons learned, ideas I wanted to remember or share with others. I stopped when I realized that I was highlighting most of the book and taking notes on every single chapter.

When I finished the book, I was left speechless. As one of Rachel's colleagues, I have admired her as a woman of extraordinary beauty and heart. I glimpsed some of what she had suffered when she shared her story from the main stage at a health and leadership conference. Until reading this book, I was unaware of the backstory, the depths of her suffering, and her monumental spiritual strength.

The power of this book is in its authenticity. We journey through the depths of Rachel and Sarah's responses to trials and tragedies, and we are not left to despair. Rather we are inspired by how Rachel and Sarah rely on the Lord and allow themselves to spiritually progress and be transformed.

I feel humbled and awe as I witness Psalm 77:14 in my work with Pure Hope Foundation: *You are the God who performs miracles; you display your power among the peoples.* I feel the same reverence and astonishment reading this important book. The God of the New Testament, the God of the Old Testament, is the God of Miracles. Our God is alive and active, is the same yesterday, today, and forever. The Smartt women open our eyes and allow us to witness the active and personal God of miracles.

Everyone needs to read this book — an offering of love, hope, and faith. The depth of the spiritual lessons learned will move the hearts of every reader.

Kathrine Lee
Life & Business Strategist
Founder of Pure Hope Foundation

Acknowledgements

Writing a memoir about love, trials, miracles, and faith was a calling that presented me with numerous challenges and obstacles that were transformed into progress because of Divine Assistance and the loving and professional support I received from many family members and friends. To them I owe my deepest gratitude.

My Father in Heaven and Savior Jesus Christ for unconditional love, divine tutoring, forgiveness, restored hope, belief, and direction.

Dave, the love of my life, for teaching me how to love, live, and matter.

My daughters: Stephanie for your gifts of compassion and authenticity; Sarah for your gifts of fun, courage, and intentional living; Megan for your gifts of adventure, love, and light-heartedness; Michelle for your gifts of innocence, service, and unwavering faith.

Stephen and Josef for bringing significance, strength, and love to our home.

Mom and Dad for providing a home where my faith was nurtured and God came first.

Ken and Earllyn for teaching our family about unconditional love.

My siblings for all the childhood memories, birthdays, encouragement, and belly laughs.

Steve, Cheryl, and Lynette for loving and encouraging Dave, for being his confidante during the good times and bad, for supporting and loving our family.

Justin Johnson for your caring friendship, encouragement, spiritual guidance, endless hours, and selfless love. Thank you for believing in and mentoring me along my toughest days.

Vicki Clarke, Pam Moore, Sherry Turner, Carol Kirkpatrick, Suzie Dean, Bethany Rooney, and Victoria Wilcox for your editing support, insight, and dear friendship.

Jose Montez for your tutoring and strong mentorship, teaching me to communicate effectively, speak to large crowds, and willingness to serve unconditionally and spontaneously.

Bryce Gibby for your brilliance and clear vision, spiritual guidance, and encouragement to Dave and our children.

Marla Fletcher and Matt Beckwith for always stopping on a moment's notice and giving of your time, talent, and energy willingly.

The late Tom Deery for believing in me when I doubted and teaching me how to be patient and overcome adversity.

Cynthia Gompers for teaching me the three secrets of communication -- to smile, come from the heart, and have fun.

Kathrine Lee for your example of deep commitment, pure compassion, faith, and friendship. Thank you for being one of my most inspirational mentors and a leader of hope and transformation. You are a woman of great faith and beauty. You have taught me to dream big, believe, and love all people without hesitation.

My Juice Plus+ Family for loyal friendships, personal growth, and providing a path that aligned with my purpose.

Jay Martin and Elton Dubose, thank you for giving me back the power to dream again and truly caring about and investing in our family.

Adidas Family for your generosity, love, encouragement, and never ending support. Scott Dallas, Ken Linden, Jamie Merriwether - you were the miracle workers in Dave's Life.

My Church Family, Community, and Neighboring Faiths for your support, fasting, mighty prayers, love of God, and eight years of unwavering service.

Sharon Thompson for being my Mother Teresa Friend, helping me trust in the Lord, picking me up when I wanted to quit, taking me to India to experience inner wealth, and being a bright example of charity and pure love of Christ.

Elizabeth Jones for your loyalty, pure love of Christ, and for your ability to mother my children like your own. You are a friend that most people only dream about.

Larry Jones, Reed and MaryAnn Gallie, Mike and Andrea Houghtaling, Rodger and Denise Purdy, Matt and Juli Beckwith, Steve and Kalleen Lund, John and Anita Marler, Tom and Kimberly Grant, Anne Myers, Gina Tilton, Ann Plauche, Sheila Nielson, Ron and Victoria Wilcox , Rich and Tammy Wonnacott, Jeff and Wendy Stebar, for teaching us true sacrifice, love and compassion, and putting our family first when we needed you.

And special thanks to

Kim Douglas for your dedication, spiritual insight, and divine wisdom. You are a transformational teacher and friend. You have taught me the value and cumulative effect of taking small steps forward to achieve the dream of writing a book while living a full and busy life. Thank you for being such a clear communicator, powerful coach, and elegant writer. Thank you for your friendship—for listening, believing in me, loving me, and pushing me to exceed beyond any limitations.

Sarah Smartt for your courage, faith, and ability to forgive. You have taught me how to love unconditionally, surrender my life and my will to the care of God, and to bounce back after tremendous trials. You see only the good and demonstrate compassion. Thank you for being my partner in writing and for the endless hours of editing, sleepless nights, walks on the bike paths, and the many belly laughs. You have inspired me to believe in myself, fill my own shoes, and believe in and receive mighty miracles.

I

1
Penny and the Persimmon Tree

Life is a journey. It is about growing, changing, and coming to terms with who and what we are, our destination, and our sacred partnership with God.
Rachel Smartt

As a child I longed to fly. Galloping bareback on Penny across the wide-open pasture, I imagined we were soaring high in the sky above our Georgia home. Penny's hooves pounded against the ground in various rhythms and patterns as we raced to our preferred spot, a favorite persimmon tree. Her deep breaths, movement, and cadence filled me with a sense of power, purpose, and peace. United as one, we were free, surmounting any problems or worries.

Before Penny came into my life, I attempted to ride the family cow after the evening feeding. I placed hay close to the fence and slid onto her back. Riding Blackie was unsafe, unpredictable, and uncomfortable. Every time I rode her, I fell or was thrown. Those hard landings had me pleading and begging my father for a horse. I received Penny, a Bay Tennessee Walker, for my thirteenth birthday.

I confided in and depended on only a few friends during early childhood. I wanted friends who were trustworthy and loyal. Penny became my faithful friend. She waited by the fence for me to return from school. She trotted alongside me as I ran toward the house where I would complete my homework and chores. No matter what challenges I faced at school, or the mood that accompanied them, Penny's whinny lifted my spirits. I treasured brushing, watering, and feeding her, all the while whispering praises and compliments to her. As I cared for Penny I learned the value of extending kindness and patience with others, including myself.

Caring for Penny also taught me responsibility. If I didn't feed her, she didn't eat. If I failed to ride her, she became wild-tempered. If I neglected to clean her hooves, she suffered from pain. I learned to understand her needs by comprehending what her eye and ear movements meant, the swishes of her tail, and the changes in her body tension. After a few years of training together, we knew each other so well that Penny recognized my unspoken commands. She understood the meaning of my slight movements. If I pressed a certain way, she took me in the appropriate direction. When I applied different pressure, she would increase her speed. She sensed my thoughts before I had a chance to say them out loud.

On our longer weekend rides, I pondered and contemplated the future and possible careers. While walking under the Georgia pines and trotting through wild dandelion fields, I simultaneously searched for solutions. During these jaunts, I would often wrestle with my self-worth, and with my purpose and place in the world. At times, when I was trying to fit in at school and home, I felt broken, lost, or displaced. I hungered for my own unique identity.

Looking into Penny's big brown eyes was like gazing into some promised future. I felt assured of my worth. While riding in the saddle or bareback, I often prayed and would experience clarity and receive answers. Although I enjoyed galloping and racing with Penny, I discovered the importance of being still and basking in the Lord's unconditional support of me. In these early years, I began planting seeds of faith and learned how to listen to whisperings of the spirit. While riding Penny, I learned to trust God and keep my heart open to His direction. Those rides cultivated the budding and blossoming of my partnership with the Savior. I started feeling more of an attraction to scripture and an appreciation of the righteous attitudes and behaviors taught at home.

On longer rides with Penny, I learned the value of our partnership, especially with respect to life's challenges. While riding Penny, I learned to dodge encounters with poisonous snakes, wild dogs, and whizzing cars. We cautiously navigated through flowing currents over uneven creek beds. Sometimes, our rides began under sunny crystal-clear skies and were interrupted by a sudden torrential Georgia downpour. During such times, I rode Penny leaning forward with my arms and legs wrapped tightly around her. My firm touch and commanding voice encouraged her homeward. Through extensive training, we grew sensitive to each other's inner beings, sounds, and impressions. We countered predicaments with skill and precision.

In retrospect, I realize my relationship with Penny served as both a tutoring ground and a foundation upon which I could grow – a foundation that served me well when I moved out West, finished high school, started college, and fell in love. I learned to listen to the voice within. I came to value my questions and develop patience as I embraced the answers that emerged. I discovered that my choices impacted my future. I began to focus on my strengths. I increased my love for others, my family, and myself. Life on earth, I realized, was a testing ground. I needed to expand my love for God and place my full trust in Him to transcend challenges, and increase my faith while navigating uncertain times and tumultuous paths.

2
Timeless Love Story

*Love is the emblem of eternity, it confounds all notion of time, offers
all memory of a beginning, all fear of an end.*
Madame de Stael

Late one afternoon after all my classes, in walked a
handsome young man wearing a red and white Ute baseball
uniform. I had been waiting for some friends inside the front
entrance of the campus student commons at the University of
Utah when I noticed him. He walked with confidence, passion,
and purpose, as if the sun followed him. He was over six feet
tall, had an athletic build, was gorgeous with thick sandy blonde
hair and neatly trimmed moustache, crystal clear blue eyes,
English nose, square forehead, and high cheekbones.

He stopped to use the pay phone adjacent to where I was
sitting and we exchanged smiles. I lowered my eyes as if
engrossed in study, but kept him in the periphery of my vision.
He put some change into the pay phone, pressed a few buttons
and waited for the call to go through. As he talked, he turned
and faced me. I pretended to be unaware of him, yet my ears
were on high alert as I attempted to eavesdrop.

He called his mother and shared details about his upcoming
baseball game, classes, and a tough homework assignment.
Then he asked about her day. He didn't rush the conversation
but took time to listen and respond in a considerate, thoughtful,

and tender way. He obviously loved and respected his mother. I was impressed with how he spoke to her, so unlike the inconsiderate way some sons talk to their mothers.

As he hung up the phone, he said, "Hi, I'm Dave. Who are you waiting for? Do you have a boyfriend?"

Startled, I looked up at him. Taken aback by his boldness, I fumbled for words and managed to respond, "I date, but I don't have any serious boyfriends in the area."

"So what's your name?"

"Rachel. And you?"

"Dave Smartt. Nice to meet you, Rachel. I hope to see you around."

He was even more attractive than I realized at first glance. I watched him walk away and smiled. Who was this strikingly attractive guy, this Dave Smartt, who just flirted with me? I had to know, so I gathered my books, hurried into one of the nearby rooms, and asked a group standing around if anyone knew him.

"Who doesn't know Dave!" said one.

"He's the head baseball pitcher for the university," answered another.

"Everyone loves Dave. He's involved in everything."

I then called one of my friends who worked at the administration building to see if she could look up Dave's class schedule. The chances of finding him on such a large campus, unless I bumped into him as he was coming out of a class or showed up for one of his baseball games, were slim.

Throughout the next few weeks I caught glimpses of Dave in large crowds but never got close enough to have another conversation. If we were supposed to connect again, I reasoned to myself, it would happen in its own due time. I continued to stay focused on school and my friends. I tried not to think about Dave.

About a month later, before Christmas break, I was studying in the back common area, a place where very few people pass through. I had just taken a bite of a crunchy granola bar when I looked up and saw Dave walk into the room. I actually choked on some of the seeds and took a swig of water to stop the coughing. I tried not to show my embarrassment. "Rachel," he said, obviously surprised to see me. He plopped down beside me, explained that he was looking for a friend and only had a few minutes before he had to head off to baseball practice. We chatted about our families, majors, and hobbies. "Interested in getting together after Christmas break?" he asked. I gave him my number. He explained that the next few weeks were filled with wedding events since his sister was getting married. "I'll call you after winter break," he promised. But Christmas break came and went without any word from Dave.

A few weeks after we all returned to school, I waited for my best friend, who attended another local college, to pick me up at the university library for a weekend away. A lush atrium in the center of the library rose up from the bottom to the top floor. I stood near a bench in the center of the first floor foyer. When I spotted Dave walking with confidence towards me, I figured he must have eyed me from above. "Hey, Rachel. I'm sorry for not calling like I said I would. I lost your number. Sure hoping you'll give me another chance," he said. I chuckled and told him I

9

wasn't going to be stood up a second time. "Awww, give me one more chance. I blew it, I realize. No dropping slips of paper with numbers on them this time," he said, chuckling.

"Well, okay then," I grinned back at him.

"How about next Saturday? I'll call you mid-week to confirm the time," he said. He thanked me when I gave him my address and phone number.

When my friend arrived, I left Dave standing in the center of the atrium. I turned around to wave and blushed seeing that his eyes were still on me. I felt giddy the rest of the day.

The next week came and went without a phone call from Dave to confirm the time. By Friday I was mad. If Dave were to call or stop by, I didn't want to be home. On Saturday morning I drove over to my aunt and uncle's house to study. They were planning to head out to run a few errands. Just before leaving, the doorbell rang. My aunt answered and called to me, "Rachel, you have a visitor." There, at the front door, stood Dave. I was shocked. It was only ten in the morning. Dave lived thirty minutes away, in another town. He explained that he drove to my home and that my parents provided him with directions so he could confirm our date in person. We agreed that he would return to pick me up that evening at six o'clock.

We chatted for about thirty minutes. "I have an idea," I said. "How about you stay and we take the horses for a ride down by the lake?" He agreed and we rode the horses, talked about our families, goals beyond graduation, hobbies, likes and dislikes, even some of our dreams. I felt a sense of calm and peace being with Dave. He was positive, interesting, and showed interest in knowing more about me.

Dave picked me up at my parent's home that evening, right on time. After introducing him to my family we were off. We drove to an American grill restaurant and then played miniature golf. Dave beat me at golf. We decided to grab some dessert at Marie Calendar's. Dave parked the car, looked at me and said, "You, Rachel, are stunningly beautiful." He then reached over and pulled me toward him. We kissed. Our kiss seemed perfectly natural, even for a first date. I wanted to hold onto the moment and make time stand still.

We practically skipped into the restaurant holding hands. Holding hands also felt natural. Why, then, were so many people in the restaurant staring at us? I excused myself and went to the Ladies Room. When I looked in the mirror I was stunned. Why had I picked the red lipstick?! Back at the table, David and I joked about the smears and laughed.

Holding his hand on the way home felt natural. Kissing him goodbye after our first date felt sacred.

In the months ahead, Dave and I shared many more laughs and continued to grow closer. I opened up and confided in him about everything, which I didn't do with everyone. Over the next two years of steady courtship, my love and admiration for him grew. Every quality I had wanted in a companion was packaged up in Dave. He was spiritual, honest, good-looking, healthy, and grateful. His social skills drew people to him. He was affectionate and courteous with everyone. The questions he asked of others showed his genuine curiosity and interest in them. His storytelling abilities, how he laughed at himself rather than others, and his optimism and zeal for life were magnetic. All of these qualities and his deep love for his family stemmed from what I admired most—his strong faith in God.

The sky was as crystal clear as Dave's blue eyes, when I looked into them on November 1, 1984. Though I don't remember all the words of the ceremony, I remember how I felt. My whole being—heart and soul—said yes. Dave and I committed to be true and faithful companions and honor our marriage above all else. Arm in arm and surrounded by family and friends, we celebrated that entire day. We enjoyed lunch, cake-cutting, and a long dinner reception. Heaven on earth was our reality.

3
And So It Begins

There are far better things ahead than any we leave behind.
C.S. Lewis

We left Salt Lake City for Denver when Dave's employers, Noxell and Cover Girl, transferred him to open up new stores in Colorado. The mile high city was our destination. Because of the move, I decided to step away from university life and start working. I landed a great job as a sales consultant for a large apartment and condo property. One of the benefits was free housing close enough to walk to work. Even though none of our family members lived in Colorado, it wasn't long before we made many friends and enjoyed settling into our new community.

A requirement of Dave's new position was that he wear a suit. His new colleagues filled him in on how to purchase designer, 100 per cent cotton, white shirts. Dave enjoyed simplicity and feeling comfortable. He had no interest in the details of fine clothing, so these conversations bored him. He managed to own only four suits during his career. His charisma made up for any lack of the so-called required fashion. He didn't need to "dress up" to feel important or get noticed. His fun-loving personality and genuine interest in others attracted everyone to him and contributed to his success in sales.

Within two years of moving, we started a family. Our first three daughters were born a couple years apart, and I enjoyed the great advantage of dedicating my efforts to being a homemaker. Both Dave and I valued motherhood. Dave wanted me to have fun with the children, and I did. I woke each morning, prepared Dave's sack lunch, including a note of appreciation for his hard work and contributions, and then focused on the day ahead, always filled with some engaging activity. I enjoyed having neighbors and friends over who were also mothers. Planning birthday parties or holiday celebrations became a creative endeavor. There were school activities, and trips to the zoo or the library. I loved being a full-time wife and mother.

Each morning Dave drove off in a company car to service accounts like K-Mart, Wal-Mart and other department stores in the Denver area. He set up displays, stocked products, worked with buyers, conducted inventories, attended training meetings, and wrote reports. More days than not, Dave returned home around four with his tie already off before he walked in the door. He spent the first hour in his home office completing all the paperwork he disliked before dinner at five. After we ate, we placed Megan in a backpack, Sarah in a stroller, and Stephanie on a bike, and walked alongside a creek to Bible Park. We noticed the Aspen trees, Colorado pines, butterflies, and flowers. Dave, a big kid at heart, imitated different Disney characters like Donald Duck and Tigger. He galloped like a horse, or pretended to be a turtle.

When Dave played with the kids, he let down all his workday goals and had fun. I, on the other hand, connected playing with setting a goal or intention. What was the skill to obtain? What was the lesson to be learned? I focused on heading to the park, providing time for the children to swing and teeter-totter, time for Dave and me to spin them on the merry-go-round. Dave frolicked on the way to the park. He had an uncanny ability to be in the moment and take advantage of the journey to a destination, amusing himself and us before we even arrived at the place I had designated for enjoyment. Walking to and visiting the park revealed our different personalities.

Just like Dave and I had our unique ways, our daughters also differed from one another. Stephanie played a particular game. When people came up to tell her how pretty she was, she stopped smiling and didn't respond. The result? They went away and left her alone. One day, after noticing this tendency, I asked her why she didn't smile and show her true self to others. She explained that she liked the attention and liked to control herself. She was a smart one.

Sarah, on the other hand, was Miss Giggles. Charming and spirited in front of everyone, including strangers, she hooted and giggled from head to toe. Her big heart was a helping heart. She made everything easier for her sister, Stephanie. She made Stephanie's bed and organized Stephanie's shoes. She even covered for her when Stephanie got in trouble.

Megan, the only child to not sit still, stopped taking naps after six months. By the age of two, she refused to wear shoes, preferring to enjoy the world barefoot. She loved clothes, and changed several times during the day, making more laundry. This child was determined to get what she wanted. I struggled to keep up with her, admiring some of the leadership qualities emerging in her.

Most nights after returning from the park, we prepared the girls for bed, read stories, and said prayers. While I cleaned the kitchen or prepared for the next day, Dave handled some laundry or housecleaning.

Friday nights were our date nights, and on occasional Saturday mornings, we took off for Vail. On the way, Dave rolled down the car window and beat his hand against the steering wheel and sang,

Colorado Rocky Mountain high
I've seen it rainin' fire in the sky
The shadow from the starlight
is softer than a lullaby
Rocky Mountain high

Sunshine on My Shoulders was another favorite of Dave's and he belted that out, too. In Vail, we rode bikes, hiked, and visited various parks. When we returned home Saturday night, we prepared for what was often the busiest day of our week – Sunday. While Dave prepared the girls for bed, I laid out the girls' Sunday dresses, gathered all the Sunday School books, and prepared snacks.

Even so, Sunday mornings were nothing short of chaotic. I felt as if I was wearing a mask walking into church. We looked picture perfect. The girls wore dresses I had made for them, with matching bows in their brushed hair. Even though I had turned on hymns at home to prepare us for a reverent atmosphere, I rushed every which way. I nursed the baby, filled the crock pot with ingredients for our dinner, dressed myself and the girls, and grabbed what I had prepared the night before —all the while reminding everyone to hurry or we'd be late. Somehow we always made it to church early, which was necessary because Dave had responsibilities prior to the service.

One day I sat on the bench with the girls and steadied my breathing. I sat tall and felt accomplished. We had made it on time. Then I glanced down and noticed Stephanie's mismatched socks, and one of Megan's shoes was missing. Was that a smudge of oatmeal on Sarah's cheek? Hardly picture perfect except perhaps from a distance. That's when I noticed Dave on the stand in the chapel looking out over the congregation. He noticed everyone in their Sunday best, without all the imperfections one can see up close. He knew, however, that most families and individuals struggled either with their own internal challenges—their "Gethsemane or Goliaths."

Church consisted of the main service, followed by Sunday school, and then age-group classes. Three hours spent at church were long for adults, and especially for small children. Some of my learning, especially when I was nursing the girls, took place in the mother's lounge or in the hallway. One Sunday late in the day, I sat in the back of the Chapel. I was striving to hear the church leader's message. My kids fidgeted, giggled, crumpled paper, and poked one another. "Heavenly Father, was it really worth all the preparation to get here?" I thought to myself. "And with all this commotion and noise in the back of the chapel, how could a visitor or anyone for that matter know whether the message spoken was true?"

Almost immediately, a prevailing spiritual impression flooded through me that no picture perfect family existed, children made noise and didn't sit still, and that was not what mattered. What mattered was that our children's souls, my soul, Dave's soul, were being nourished. Even if our children did not yet understand and only took in little drops of what was taught each Sunday, we were deepening their faith.

Over the course of that year, while listening to a strong spiritual message, a song or testimony at church, I often noticed my children look up and become quiet. In those moments, I believed the Spirit of God was touching them. By going through all the chaos of preparing for church, by making what felt like super-human efforts most Sundays, we were making a difference in the lives of our children.

We returned home at noon, hungry, and ready for our crock pot Sunday dinner. After eating, we either watched a movie or took a nap. Dave and I implemented special Sunday rules for our family: no playing with friends, no shopping, and no videos that weren't church-related. Once a month following Sunday dinner, our family visited and tried to uplift a person in need. The girls presented drawings or small gifts. Dave and I wanted the girls to learn how to serve as the Lord did, and care for those who needed an emotional boost, an encouraging word, or love.

Sunday naptime at three o'clock was sacred for Dave and me. The girls knew that no knocking on the bedroom door was allowed. They could rest, play, or read while we rested after a busy week. This provided Dave and I time to talk, love one another, and recharge.

At the close of our day, we gathered together to read from the Scriptures and held a family prayer. In unity, we bowed our heads in appreciation for all the blessings from our Heavenly Father. Life was good, even with all the chaos, dirty dishes, and loads of laundry.

4
Second Honeymoon Hurricane

Gratitude bestows reverence, allowing us to experience
unexpected moments of our lives
that changed how we experience and view the world.
John Milton

Resting on a small pristine beach, hiking through lush green foliage, and inhaling the tropical flowers were all part of the plan for our ten-day second honeymoon that September of 1989. Six months prior to our visit to Water Island, the smallest of the main U.S. Virgin Islands, we started planning the trip. Inhabited by a small population of only 100, the island consisted of only fifty acres of land. Historically, Water Island was once populated by several diverse groups of Indians, pirates, slaves, and the British Government—and had since been groomed for tourists. We decided to lodge off the beaten path, visit plantation ruins, and snorkel to explore shipwrecks and coral reefs, where the marine life was plentiful with an abundance of fish, turtles and manta rays.

None of the pictures we had seen or read about compared to the actual beauty of the island. We soaked in the scenery on the ten-minute ferryboat ride from the main island to Water Island. The crystal clear water was calm. Not a single cloud dotted the sky and none hovered in the horizon. We were told about a hurricane warning but felt certain the storm would travel around the island, leaving us unaffected and our vacation memorable in the ways we imagined.

Residential homes, quaint apartments, and villas converted from former army barracks owned by the British government dotted the landscape. We had settled in our small apartment. Because few of the ten other apartments were occupied, we felt like a king and queen of our own private island and couldn't wait to unpack and begin our exploration, swimming, and fun.

The first couple of days we woke early and raced off to explore. We inhaled the fragrance of red hibiscus flowers. We rested on the immaculate white sandy beach. We snorkeled and admired brilliantly colored fish and coral. We ate delicious food.

Throughout the third day our uneasiness heightened when news reporters announced that Hugo had increased to a level three hurricane and had changed its course. The eye of the storm took aim directly on Water Island. One hundred and thirty-five mile winds, tempestuous waters, and mountainous waves could result in massive destruction. We rushed out to the store for food and supplies. The shelves were almost bare. On our way back, we snapped photos of the dark gray clouds stretching across the entire sky and the trees and foliage that whipped about by the gales. The waves thrashed the coastal rocks.

We stopped to speak to an elderly woman boarding up her home on the coast. A widow with no family nearby and no insurance, she was afraid. Because our place was only twenty feet away from her home, we invited her to stay with us. She shook her head and said she wanted to remain in her own home.

Dave, enthralled with how the storm was developing, began to capture the progression and some of the early destruction on our camcorder. I decided to watch from inside where it was safe and dry. The storm surge was predicted to reach twenty-one feet. I worried for the woman we had met. Would her house withstand the hurricane? And what about us?! Would we make it out of here? Would we make it back to our daughters?

Dave rushed in the door. "Tree uprooted," he said, offering a worried laugh.

By nightfall, we lost all modern conveniences—no water, no cool air, no electricity. The storm raged on. We went to bed, held hands, and prayed to God to watch over and protect us. The roar and rumble of the hurricane resembled ten airplanes taking off at the same time. The banging, crashing, and clattering—worse than anything I had ever heard in my life—was followed by an eerie silence. We had been told we would experience intervals of massive destruction and utter silence.

The second round began and the beating of the storm increased. The wind uprooted more trees. Branches flew through the air and hit against the apartment. The wind peeled back nearby roofs. Neighbors screamed about the rain coming in. We knew it was only a matter of time before our roof would be next. Sure enough, the winds stripped off our metal roof from one end to the other.

Finally the nightmare came to an end. The sun rose. We headed out to survey the damage. Even though the blue sky looked like it did the first day we arrived, the island was unrecognizable. Ships that stood safely in the harbor were scattered in pieces all the way to the top of St. Thomas Island. Trees were uprooted. Dead sea animals, large and small, were sprawled all over the island. The stench and heat intensified, making us nauseous. Debris, wood, seaweed, and rubble filled the private beach where we spent our first couple of days.

We spotted a young Puerto Rican boy walking around, completely naked, crying out "Master. Master." Despite his broken English, we managed to learn that he and his employer had decided to battle the hurricane alone. Even though advised to seek shelter by authorities, they remained on their boat, hoping to outsmart the storm. Winds and waves tossed the boy out of the boat onto shore and knocked him unconscious. He pointed out pieces of the boat on the beach. We joined the search team and spent hours looking for his employer. The team decided to give up, figuring that the boy's "master" had died at sea or was unrecognizable under all the rubble on the beach.

Heartbroken that no one could find the man, Dave and I joined the young boy to continue to search for him. "God, help us find him. You know where he is. Guide us," I uttered to myself. We walked along. Within moments I looked down in the rubble. Even though I had walked by this same spot many times, something was different. What I perceived earlier as a coconut and sticks was not what I thought. "Dave," I called out. "Come here. Check this out. I think this is a head. An arm." At first, Dave shook his head, but as he moved, he closed his eyes, dropped his head, and sighed. Though grateful to find the remains of the young boy's master, we had heartbreaking news to deliver.

Within 24 hours, everyone on Water Island was evacuated. We were allowed only one phone call to let our families know we were safe. We searched for another place to stay until we could fly back home. The only hotels that were not completely destroyed doubled their prices. We asked another couple, also tourists, if they wanted to share a room. They agreed. We spent the next seven days together, mostly watching the news. Because of the unfortunate looting and crime common after disasters, the government ordered martial law.

Finally, we were able to fly back home. When we landed in Florida, we got to our knees and kissed the ground. We had witnessed and survived one of the greatest storms in history. Sick with fever, dehydrated and exhausted, we were grateful to be alive. We came home with an abundant reverence for life, our children and our family.

5
The Race

*Strength doesn't come from what you can do, it comes from
overcoming the things you once thought you couldn't.*
Rikki Rogers

Each one of our daughters owned several pairs of tennis
shoes, compared to the single pair I owned growing up in a
large family of eight. The new family I had created was half the
size, and Dave had received a significant offer to work for
Adidas Shoe Company. After eight years of living in the mile
high city, we moved our family to Peachtree City, Georgia. Here,
our daughter, Michelle, was born, and there was another set of
feet to fit with shoes, which Dave loved.

Dave taught us all about the various categories of athletic
shoes. There were shoes for walking, hiking, jogging, running,
and cross-training. He made sure our shoes included the right
cushioning, flexibility, and stability. Comfort, traction, style, and
correct fit—all of this mattered to Dave. He was an expert.
Though he didn't care much about brand names or being in
style, all of those preferences vanished when it came to wearing
Adidas shoes and apparel. He was proud of working for Adidas.

Dave and I both grew up participating in athletic and extra-
curricular activities. We wanted our children to have the same
privileges and opportunities. We encouraged our children to
take music lessons and to select and participate in one sport. We

believed that playing sports fostered the development of virtues, such as determination, respect, cooperation, resiliency, self-confidence, and endurance. We wanted our children to learn how to create healthy friendships, work as part of a team, and develop the capacity to reflect on the lessons that come from both winning and losing. We also made the commitment to support and cheer each other on by showing up for games and performances.

During fifth grade, our eldest daughter Stephanie signed up to run a 5K in Peachtree City. Dave, equipped with all of the knowledge he had from working for Adidas, helped prepare Stephanie for this event. He ordered not just one but two pairs of shoes for her to try. He tested her running gait. He measured her feet, making sure they were big enough so her toes could wiggle and snug enough that her heel remained inside the shoes without slipping out. He often re-laced the shoes, beginning with the farthest eyelets and applying even pressure as he laced the shoes from bottom to top in crisscross fashion. Then he had Stephanie walk, sprint, and then run up and down the driveway. This is how he analyzed her gait, pronation, and foot patterns.

I never knew buying shoes was such a science and an art. When I grew up, I wore four-striped tennis shoes. When I made the high school All-Star Basketball Team, I earned enough money to purchase my very own white Adidas shoes with three red stripes—at last a name brand with the number of stripes that meant I was *cool*. I never considered cushioning, pronation, how the shoes fit, or how to lace them.

The day before the race Dave and I reminded Stephanie of particular running tips, like relaxing and breathing when she ran. Dave took Stephanie out to the store to buy her Quench chewing gum and her favorite breakfast bar. He also bought high performance running socks and running clothes. After dinner, before we gathered for family prayers, I made Dave promise he would not excite the girls at bedtime, as usually happened. The girls loved Daddy's bedtime routine of fluffing the pillows and sheets and giggling and tickling. He agreed, realizing that Stephanie needed her sleep. After our family prayers, I returned to the kitchen to fill water bottles and prepare healthy snacks for the next day. Dave guided the girls upstairs to read them a bedtime story and turn out the lights.

Morning came all too fast. We drove to the Frederick Brown Amphitheater. The gigantic parking lot was perfect for the race. We joined the long line of people to pick up Stephanie's registration materials. Dave took Stephanie to the starting line and remained with her. Because she was wide-eyed with excitement and some anxiety, he took her through a series of stretches. I positioned Michelle, just one, on my hip and led Sarah and Megan along the scenic course framed with Georgia pines. Michelle, enjoying the ride on my hip, giggled and smiled as we marked out the best spots to cheer from the sidelines. I placed some of our belongings at the beginning of the race and some mid-way, so we could encourage Stephanie at different times throughout her run.

Back near the starting line, both Dave and I suggested to Stephanie that she focus on her own breathing, set her own pace, and avoid the common pitfalls of many runners—starting out too fast and wasting a lot of energy, which results in losing ground in the middle and at the end of the race where the most energy is needed. The start pistol fired and the race began. The pack of runners sped off, each endeavoring to find their pace and rhythm.

We ran back and forth to different spots on the course, cheering for Stephanie. Toward the front of the pack, she kept a great pace throughout. Toward the end of the course with the crowds cheering on both side of the road, Stephanie struggled up a hill. Her gait was steady and she managed to keep up with the strongest runners. Right before she turned for the straightaway to the finish line, she slipped on gravel and tripped right in front of us.

Dave ran over to console her and checked out her knee that was skinned and bleeding. Other runners passed her by. I could read her expression. She was ready to quit. I overheard Dave say that she didn't have to finish. "You aren't quitting," I shouted from the sideline. "Get up, Stephanie. You're a finisher. You're not quitting. You have come too far. You can do this. No turning back. Go. You can do this. Go!"

Other supporters and parents fell silent and stared at me. Dave shot me a glance, one I knew and translated as "lighten up." He often chided me that I was way too serious when it came to playing sports. But I valued the lessons I learned from athletic experiences. Yes, I got emotional with races. I had run track. I had loved the exhilaration of competition, fighting the inner chatter and the voice that said, "Give up. You can't do this." I was proud of myself for not listening to that negativity and pushing past pain. Though I had wanted to quit many times, I knew the positive results of not doing so. My senior year in high school, I qualified for the Utah State Track Meet in the one-mile event. I ran my best time and held the track record for over ten years following high school graduation.

Stephanie could either receive comfort and quit or kick past the pain and finish. She had a decision to make. Surprising everyone, even herself, she got up, shook off the gravel, gritted her teeth, and put on her strong face. Some of the parents glared at me. I didn't care. She took off running down the hill towards the finish line with tears streaming down her face. She gave it all she had, kicked it in high gear, and finished strong, and without excuses.

A year later our daughter Sarah participated in a triathlon. Due to bad weather, rain washed off her race markings. An official ordered her to ride her bike three additional times around a three-mile route. After completing the bike route, she had to run one mile to the finish line. The storm could have ruined everything. The unfairness of riding an extra three miles could have caused Sarah to quit. And she did indeed want to quit. Stephanie, though, wouldn't let her. She ran up to Sarah, grabbed her hand, and ran alongside her all the way to the finish line. Stephanie helped Sarah discover that life isn't always fair and to keep pressing forward anyway. The one who fails is the one who quits.

Years later, Stephanie wrote me a letter thanking me for pushing her to finish that race and not give up. She learned that when obstacles and challenges occur, she had a decision to make, whether to stay knocked down or to get up and continue.

6
Tutoring Sessions

I believe the first test of a truly great man is in his humility.
John Ruskin

Dave and I received the thrilling news that we were expecting our fourth child. I dealt with the first three months of fatigue and morning sickness by focusing on my joyful longing for this next baby. Would the Lord bless us with a boy or a girl? I would be happy either way. A healthy baby was what mattered, a new life we would be blessed to bring into this wonderful world, a beautiful soul I could teach, love, and hold.

At the outset of my second trimester, I miscarried. I didn't have complications with previous pregnancies, so the loss stunned and devastated me. Had I done something to cause this? Was I eating right? Getting enough sleep? I tried to carry on, smile, and play games with my daughters, but I felt such emptiness. I wept in the shower. I struggled to prepare meals. I could barely button my own shirt. I just wanted to sleep. Even praying was hard, but I tried.

One morning Dave, pressed for time, asked if I was well enough to drop him off at the airport. He was behind in leaving for a business trip. Instead of parking his car and racing for the terminal, getting dropped off would give him the time advantage he needed. His request was a simple and routine thing, but in that moment I felt like I was being asked to climb a steep mountain.

I managed to get out of bed and put on a bathrobe. The older girls had left for school. I buckled Megan in the back seat. Dave drove through the fog and rain to the airport. When we arrived, I kissed him goodbye, got in the driver's seat, and headed back home. Just before turning onto the ramp for the freeway, Megan asked if she could sit in the passenger seat next to me. "Okay, but hurry. You need to fasten your seatbelt before we get onto the freeway." She climbed up front just as I made a sharp right turn. I didn't realize that I was going too fast for the wet road. We slid and headed straight into a five-foot cement wall and Megan wasn't buckled in. "Please God, this is it. Take over," I cried. Then I held my breath and froze. We banged into the wall. Glass exploded and shattered. Then silence enveloped us.

Stunned and dazed, I looked down at Megan, my little girl, in my lap. She was shaken up but without a single scratch or bruise. The force of gravity should have thrown her *forward*. Instead, she flew sideways, side-flipped, and landed on her pillow in my lap. I was mystified. The glass from all the windows of the van was blown out. Why hadn't we flown through the windshield when we hit the wall head on? I thanked God. This was nothing short of a miracle.

I reached over and buckled Megan in the passenger seat. I needed to move the van before any other cars came around the one-way curve. A rear-end collision, another accident, was the last thing I needed. I was in my nightgown. I couldn't even begin to fathom getting out of the car to talk to strangers, and police officers.

"You already performed one miracle. Now I need another miracle. Please, Heavenly Father, help this van start and get us home." Beads of sweat dotted my forehead. My hair was a mess.

But I let out a "thank you," when the van started to my amazement and relief. I drove with the utmost care onto the freeway, uttering, "O Father, guide me." My hands gripped the steering wheel. Megan, normally talkative, stared out of the vehicle in silence. "I need your prayers, Megan," I said. "I need your prayers, too."

Forty minutes later, we pulled safely into our driveway, exhausted and still shaking. Our van was demolished. It needed a junkyard. But that didn't matter. I held onto Megan. My only thought was *what if something had happened to her?*

Back inside, I telephoned a friend who was a car mechanic. He came right over. Shocked by the visible damage, he loaded what was left of the van onto his tow truck. In less than an hour, he called. "I can't believe you made it home. I can't believe you drove that van home. I'm shocked you made it home."

"Why are you so stunned?" I asked.

"Because the steering rack is completely cracked in half. You had NO steering and you drove all the way home."

I was speechless. I sensed that it was the hand of God protecting us. God was in the driver seat. God had helped us avoid what could have been. Surviving this accident was a miracle. But. . . what if, what if my little girl had gone through the windshield?

Shortly after that, Dave's parents were in town for a brief visit. We made reservations to try out a reputable restaurant in the city. We decided to use valet parking, something we hadn't done before. After a delicious dinner, we gave our ticket to the valet driver who went to retrieve the car. We waited. And waited. And waited. Finally, he returned, shaking his head, frowning. "I've looked everywhere. The car is nowhere to be found," he said. "I think it's been stolen."

"Stolen," we all responded, almost simultaneously. How could that have happened in a valet parking lot?

But it had. We filled out a police report, drove home in a rented car, and received word three weeks later that the car had been located on a back road on the other side of town.

Prior to the miscarriage, the accident, and the stolen car, I had accepted a new position at church working with youth. To prepare, I had begun several weeks of serious study. I came across some Scriptures and an article on how humility is an essential virtue for coming to know the Savior. In my private prayers, I asked Heavenly Father to teach me about humility so that I could become more like Christ. One evening, I asked Dave how one obtains humility. He chuckled and replied, "Through life experiences!"

What was I to learn from a sudden miscarriage, crashing into a cement wall, driving home without steering, and having our car stolen? Was Heavenly Father trying to teach me something about humility? Was He trying to help me share with youth in our church about the Savior's life, love, and mission?

These back-to-back experiences were just the start of things that shaped and humbled me. They helped me understand how my life, my possessions, and even my trials were tutoring tools from on high. I sensed that God desired to bring me back to Him so that I could become entirely dependent on Him above any other person or thing and completely trust in His plan for me and my family. He was there for me when I cried out after miscarrying, when I drove through the fog, and faltered on the road, risking my daughter's life and my own. He was there for us when our car was stolen. He was there in those stunning moments. I knew deep in my soul the Savior's promise -- that no one is forgotten by Him.

7

Angel Shell

Find out where joy resides,
and give it a voice far beyond singing.
For to miss the joy is to miss all.
Robert Louis Stevenson

Just shy of midnight on October 19, 1995, I gave birth to our fourth daughter, Michelle, at the Georgia Baptist Medical Center. Labor and delivery for my first three children lasted about twelve hours. Michelle arrived in half the time. Dave and I both agreed that Michelle was our angel. We felt overwhelmed with love and gratitude for the sacred responsibility of partnering with God to bring one of his precious spirits into the world.

Even though we were exhausted, we couldn't sleep. Giving birth is like running a marathon. We had reached the finish line of that race by delivering our fourth daughter. Those moments of welcoming and getting to know our new baby were more important than sleep.

After holding and kissing our newborn, I handed Dave our tightly-bundled baby so I could take a picture in front of the large window and brightly lit night. The view of Atlanta's city lights and stars in the dark sky enhanced our feelings. An infinite amount of love flowed from Dave to Michelle. He stroked his cheek against hers and rocked her. We treasured

Michelle's beautiful blue eyes and rose petal cheeks. We stroked her thick sandy blonde hair and marveled at her perfectly formed lips, button nose, and tiny fingernails. We listened to her soft breathing. All the little details of perfection were reflected in her—the creation and handiwork of our loving Father in Heaven. "Angel-Shell," David announced, the nickname we decided upon for our youngest. I wept and thanked Dave for being such a great father and husband. He expressed his love and appreciation for me, recognizing the pain of birth and the sacrifice that devoted mothering required. We bowed our heads in a prayer and thanked God for our marriage, our children, our deepened love, and our commitment to one another and to family life.

Back home, we resumed our family routine with one extra precious child. The first night after our three oldest were asleep, I went to check on Michelle in her room. I panicked. Where could she be? She was not in her crib. Noticing Dave's office light downstairs, I figured he must have Michelle. He did not. We hurried upstairs and checked our other children's bedrooms. There she was. We found Michelle, barely visible, in the same bed with Sarah. Sarah had her arms around her and held her like she was a baby doll. They looked so peaceful together, and we chuckled. However cute, I didn't feel comfortable with Michelle as a fragile newborn being lifted from her crib by Sarah. We gently explained to Sarah that Michelle was too small to be carried around like a doll. She could only hold her with permission.

During this time I reflected deeply on my life, especially on my role as a wife and mother, which I considered a sacred calling. I felt committed to being the best wife and supportive mother I could. I read numerous books and listened to many tapes about marriage and parenting. Appreciative that I was able to stay home, I devoted all my attention to helping our children grow strong physically, emotionally, scholastically, and especially spiritually.

I cherished "special time" with my little girls before they went to bed, a ritual that I started when they were small. I shared with each of them at least one positive behavior or characteristic they demonstrated during that day and reminded them how much I loved them. Since parenting involved chaos, imperfections, mistakes, squabbles, spills—an incredibly messy process, taking time to focus on what went right resulted in miraculous, time-stopping moments. We reflected together and bonded deeply.

Dave and I felt blessed beyond measure. We loved being parents and enjoyed placing our children's interests and activities at the center of our lives. We had treasured friends, a loving family, and a beautiful home. Dave also received a promotion to an advanced position. Our life felt absolutely perfect. We had been given everything we ever dreamed of having.

8
Wake Up Call

*... the tender mercies of the Lord are over all
those whom he hath chosen,
because of their faith, to make them mighty
even unto the power of deliverance.*
Nephi

The first symptoms were heart palpitations and a sudden rise in blood pressure. Dave grew pale. On sudden occasions, sweat didn't drip but poured from him, even in cool places. A pain deep in his right shoulder throbbed. Was it arthritis from all the years of pitching? Stress from all the travel involved with his work?

Dave dismissed the symptoms and avoided scheduling an appointment with the doctors. He continued on with family and work routines, until one sleepless night. Dave was in Portland, Oregon on a business trip. The pain in his right shoulder that had annoyed him became unbearable. He began sweating for no apparent reason. He leaned against a wall in his hotel room and tried to breathe the pain away. He didn't sleep the entire night. The next morning, still in agony, he drove himself to the closest emergency room in a rental car. A physician ordered a panel of tests, which included extensive blood work. Everything came back normal.

A week later when Dave returned home ten pounds lighter and wrestling with a variety of symptoms, we went to our family doctor and asked for more tests. The doctor didn't think we needed to do anything because Dave was young, muscular, athletic—the picture of health. But we sensed something had to be causing these unusual symptoms and insisted on a CAT scan. The doctor relented.

A day later we were called back to the doctor's office to go over the results. Rather than sitting in the waiting room with those who had checked in before us, we were led into what we thought would be an examining room. Instead, the doctor invited us into his private office. He pointed to the leather sofa and then to a small refrigerator, asking if we wanted a soda. We declined and sat down. The doctor proceeded to hold up a scan in front of the window. The light from outside illuminated the picture. He took a deep breath. He was silent for a moment. "Well," he began and then pointed to Dave's kidney, "There's a large mass on top of the kidney. It's the size of a grapefruit."

I reached for Dave's hand. My heart burned. If I hadn't been sitting, I would have collapsed.

"What do you mean by a mass?" Dave asked.

"There's a large tumor. This is a rare tumor, and I don't want you to be too alarmed until we have the results of further tests. Ninety per cent of these tumors are benign. That's the good news."

After additional tests, we received the devastating news that Dave had pheochromocytoma, a rare adrenal cancer. Dave was only thirty-seven years old. We had four little girls. We were just beginning our lives. How could this be? How could Dave, who was so healthy, get cancer?

After the initial shock, we decided to fight this diagnosis by starting with prayer and reaching out for the support of our church friends. Our church leader, and several other men from our congregation, came to our home to find Dave and me clinging to one another on the sofa. My whole body trembled. I could barely breathe. Dave sat in the middle of the room to receive the blessing. I sat all alone on the couch anxiously ready to receive God's guidance. My ears and heart were open.

When our leaders and friends laid their hands on Dave's head and spoke the words of the blessing, I felt as if they were laying their hands on my head, too. I sensed a warm, spiritual water spread from the top of my head through every part of my body. This tangible substance traveled through every vein and artery, to the tips of my fingers and the tips of my toes. I felt it enter my lungs and relax my breathing. An indescribable and exquisite peace flooded my entire being. A spiritual calm extinguished all the trembling and worries.

At the same time, we could feel and hear a sound, something like wind rushing through our house. We had never experienced this before. A dear friend who was helping put the girls to bed while Dave was receiving the blessing felt a warm wind or tangible, peaceful force pass through her body and rush into the girls' rooms. She said that sensation was the most spiritual force she had ever experienced. She knew the power of God was flowing through the house and giving comfort and protection to everyone who resided within.

Later I found two Scriptures that captured our experience: *"And suddenly there came a sound from heaven as of a rushing mighty wind, and it filled all the house where they were sitting"* (Acts 2:2) and *"let thy house be filled, as with a rushing mighty wind, with thy glory"* (Doctrine and Covenants 109:37). This rushing and mighty wind, this guidance from God Himself, on the day of the blessing, extinguished all the trembling and worries. My soul, open and receptive, sensed that God was trying to let me know that even though doctors would provide no hope, we would find hope.

9

The Devastating Truth

You never know how strong you are
until being strong is all you have.
Anonymous

Dave took off work for about three months so we could determine the best options and begin treatment. Local physicians urged us to schedule surgery right away. Hopefully, we would find out through surgery that the cancer had not metastasized. Since too few doctors had experience treating this rare cancer, most only reading about pheochromocytoma in textbooks, we decided to fly to the National Institute of Health in Maryland. We wanted the best surgeons to perform the surgery at a top hospital.

Dave's parents flew in from Utah to watch the girls. We began to map out plans so that Dave and I could spend a month in Maryland for Dave to recover after the surgery. While Dave and his Dad made the initial drive to Maryland in order for me to use the vehicle while there, I wrote out the extensive schedule for the upcoming month involving all the girls' various activities. I went over all the details with my mother-in-law before flying to Maryland to join Dave and my father-in-law.

The day before surgery I arrived and remained at Dave's side. We clung to one another. Though fear coursed through our very veins, we tried to have faith, stay calm, and remain positive.

About 7 p.m. a doctor came in to prep Dave for surgery scheduled the following morning. He explained that the operation would take all day, was very risky, and would be followed by an estimated hospital stay of one month. Several additional doctors entered the room. One of them asked the doctor in the room to leave. None of the remaining doctors smiled. They all looked sober. The head doctor walked over to Dave, who looked up from the hospital bed. "I don't have good news, Dave," he began. "We are not going to be able to operate as planned. The x-rays show that the cancer has spread throughout your body and bones. Unfortunately, there is nothing left for us to do. Traditional treatments won't improve the situation."

There was a long silence. We struggled to comprehend the words. One of the other doctors invited us to talk with a patient who had this kind of cancer.

"Are you. . ." Dave struggled for words. "Are you sending me home to die?"

The head doctor who had been doing most of the talking looked down. He paused. "I am not sending you home to die, but to live... to live the best you can for as long as you can.... approximately six months."

After all the doctors left the room, we were speechless, all of us trying to understand the devastating news. I hugged Dave. My father-in-law and I wept. Our sobs filled the white sterile room. For the first time since I had known Dave, he let out a wail.

Later, I managed to walk down the hallway to call my parents. I felt numb and dizzy and what I never expected to feel—hopeless, like I was suffocating. Dave loved life. He wanted to live. I wanted him to live. All I could manage to utter was "O Father." In that state of utter despair, I knew I was not alone. I sensed an outpouring of the Spirit, and felt as if I were being carried down the hall in the heavenly hands of my Maker.

"This is going to work out," I consoled myself at the end of that long walk. "Dave is going to fight, win, and live." I dialed the phone number of my parents and the tears flooded back. I struggled to get out the words, to share what the doctors had conveyed.

10

Back Home

You gain strength, courage, and confidence with every experience in which you really stop to look fear in the face.
Eleanor Roosevelt

Two days later, emotionally battered, we drove from Maryland back home to Georgia, crying most of the way. We were so grateful and blessed to have Dave's father with us giving us comfort and hope. We cried during the day and endured sleepless nights. Without direction, we were terrified of the future and frozen with fear.

When we arrived home, Dave struggled to get out of the car. He was the king of our house, the protector, and the provider. Usually fun-loving and energizing, he was now thin, pale, and weak. And he was heartbroken. He didn't know how he would face our little girls. He worried about how they might react.

We walked in the house where some of our dearest friends, family, and daughters were gathered around the kitchen table eating a snack. They had cleaned our house, mowed the grass, and prepared food for our arrival. Still, the air felt thick. No one quite knew what to do or say. We were trying to be brave, pretend that all would be well, but would it?

I could sense fear in the eyes of our three oldest daughters, and sense it in their frozen dispositions. Stephanie, Sarah,

Megan—only nine, eight, and six—hadn't been told anything except that their Dad was not feeling well and might need to have surgery. Before we left for Maryland, I had explained that their daddy couldn't jump on the trampoline or play in the yard, so they shouldn't ask him. I was especially worried because Dave's blood pressure rose over 300 on a few different occasions, and the doctors had expressed concern about a heart attack. Because he was an athlete, never smoked or drank, and had a strong heart, he had survived those previous occasions. But we didn't want to test our luck.

"Daddy! Daddy! Daddy! Home," Michelle squealed, breaking the thick and silent atmosphere. Dave and I let out a sigh. Michelle's one-year-old innocence, curiosity, and fun-loving playfulness were what our family needed.

We thanked our friends for all of their help. They understood that we wanted time to ourselves and to be alone with the girls. After they left, we gathered the children around in the front room. Stephanie, Sarah, and Megan sat on the couch, all holding hands. Their big round eyes seemed to be pleading for answers. They looked at each other and shrugged their shoulders as if they didn't know what was up. "Are we moving?" Stephanie asked. "Did Dad lose his job?" Though I tried to hide my emotions, fear and sadness were written all over my face. Dave was more composed but could barely manage to speak

"Girls, you know that I have not been feeling well," Dave finally began. "The doctors have been running tests on me at the hospital, and they found something."

There was a long silence.

"I have cancer and the doctors haven't given me very long to live."

Each daughter, except our youngest, struggled to deal with the news. Stephanie stared at us with no emotional expression, numbed with fear. Sarah went to her bedroom and wanted to be alone. She began organizing her drawers and personal space as she tried to process her emotions by sorting. Megan, who was active, energetic, and talkative, sat on the couch. She stared into space and cried. Michelle continued to play. She wanted to swing and jump on the trampoline. She wanted to get on her dad's shoulders and play "bungee."

Our daughters had never had to deal with serious illness or unexpected loss before. Years later they looked back and reflected with more insight. Recently, Sarah wrote about that day, "My heart sank. Everything else that he said was a blur. I didn't exactly know what cancer was, but I knew it wasn't good. I stared off into space and felt numb to emotion. I then heard Mom ask, 'Sarah, did you hear? Dad is sick.' I didn't want to hear it. He was my Dad! Who would protect me? Who would sing the Zip-a-Dee-Doo-Dah song? Who would make my toast just the way I liked? I rushed upstairs to my bedroom and distracted myself. I avoided thinking too much about it by carrying on with daily life."

After unpacking, we took our girls on a golf cart ride in an attempt to escape the pain of our new reality. We offered half a wave to our neighbors. If only we could be invisible. Even though we felt loved and cherished by our friends, all the attention was uncomfortable. We wanted and needed some alone time.

In the days ahead, Dave and I tried to appear and carry on in our *normal* ways. I mustered up all my strength to keep a happy face. For the sake of Dave and the children, I tried to keep my feelings in check, but all too often I felt overpowered by my grief. I ran out to the car or to our bedroom to cry in private.

Dave and I drew closer together, every moment seeming like the last. One day we drove to the store and afterward stopped to grab a bite to eat. We ordered and sat down with our lunch. We took one look at each other and broke into tears. Without taking a single bite, we left our food on the table. Even romance ended in tears.

We didn't know which way to turn. With as much sincerity as we had, we pleaded, even bargained, with the Lord. Dave loved life more than I did. I couldn't bear to see him suffer. "Heavenly Father, give me the cancer. Give me this pain. Let Dave live," I begged God in private prayer. Later, I came to realize I could not make that kind of sacrifice. Only the Lord could provide comfort, relief, and ultimate healing.

II

11
Lost and Found

If God answers your prayer, he increases your faith,
if God delays your prayer he increases your patience,
if God doesn't answer your prayer,
he is preparing the BEST for you.
unknown

After Dave's diagnosis, he took a leave from work. We contemplated and discussed the best and worst-case scenarios. We researched leading doctors and protocols for this rare cancer. Typically, Dave oozed confidence—in the forcefulness of his voice, his carriage, his very presence. Rather than succumb to the death sentence given by the doctors, he was struggling to survive the doctors' predictions. Doing so was difficult because Dave's symptoms and pain hit new highs and his immune system new lows. He lost weight. His energy plummeted. The bone pain increased. He broke out in bouts of profuse sweating. He struggled to eat and sleep.

During this already nerve-wracking time, Dave lost his wallet. This occurred a few days before his birthday. We ransacked the house several times. We looked under cushions, rummaged through our vehicles, and scoured dressers and drawers. We spent whole days canceling credit cards, obtaining a new driver's license, and replacing missing business cards. For three long weeks the family searched. We prayed. We fasted. Still, there was no sign of the wallet.

Try as I might, I could not shift my mood into a festive mode for Dave's approaching birthday. I was depressed, angry, and sad. I descended to a new low. "Heavenly Father, are you there?" I began to wonder. "Do you answer every child's prayer? Why can't I feel you?" My cries to the Lord didn't relieve me of feeling lost and alone.

On October 9th, Dave's birthday, I dragged myself to the local department store before dinner and purchased a new leather wallet. Afterwards, I drove to the bank to withdraw cash to place in the wallet, adding a little extra value. On my way back home in bumper-to-bumper four o'clock afternoon traffic, I turned left at a major intersection. As a storm brewed on the horizon, the wind picked up. Autumn leaves twirled and spun around the cars and embankment. As I drove, I broke down. I was sad, frustrated, and angry. I doubted God's guidance. I questioned His love for Dave. Where was His support? "I know you know where that wallet is. Don't you care about Dave? I need you! Where are you?"

No sooner had I spoken those words than I looked into the rear-view mirror and saw white pieces of paper fluttering in the wind. A surging rush of the Spirit swelled throughout my body. I pressed on the brakes and merged into the right lane. I glanced in the rear view mirror. Slips of paper fluttered alongside the road. A strong impression of peace and love flowed into my heart, along with these words: *I am completely aware of Dave and the circumstances you are in. I am taking care of him just like I have protected and preserved his wallet on top of this van for over three weeks during travel, rain, wind, and washings. Be still. Know that I am God and that I love you.*

I pulled the van to a complete stop. I stepped out of the van and looked up to the roof of the vehicle. The black leather wallet flapped open in the wind. Obviously, Dave had placed it there weeks before while putting the children in the van. How had it stayed up on the top of the van without falling off or getting damaged?

Humbled, I bowed in reverence and gratitude. I was ashamed of my doubts and impatience. Up until that point, my prayers were not a conversation with the Lord but an illusion of communication. My pleas were monologues with Him, reflecting my frustration with the situation. Even then, when I was more into talking than listening, my Heavenly Father continued to teach me about His love and power. Even then, He showed me He was alive, aware, and real as He reached me that windy day. I promised Him I would respect His timing and trust His divine presence.

I floated home elated, unable to contain my emotions. I soared into the house and shared the story of the lost-and-found wallet with Dave and the girls. Dave jumped up, clapped his hands and shouted YES, and then reached to give me a tight embrace. The children squealed. Dave and our older daughters took off to see if they could retrieve some of the important lost papers. Even though the traffic was heavy and the wind continued to gust due to an approaching storm, they located all of Dave's business cards and most of the money.

Our family's faith grew as we took time to reflect on the tender mercy of the Lord in this and other situations. Even when we doubted His presence, He never forgot us. He knew the smallest details of our lives. He was completely present during the days we dreaded, the days we doubted, the days we wept, and the days we embraced.

12
New Normal

At some point you have to let go of what you thought should happen and live with what is happening.
Unknown

Almost overnight we grew more mindful about our hours and days together. We became intentional master schedulers, penciling onto the calendar our various responsibilities and memory-making family activities. Dave made a list of all the various activities he had promised the girls. We did not delay. No more sleepwalking through life or paying half attention. Our senses were intensified. What would be our next vacation? When was the next school function or soccer game? On weekends, we deliberately unplugged from phones, TV, and computers. Instead, we explored a small unfamiliar town, visited a "forbidden" ice cream shop, and enjoyed a treat. Even Dave took one or two licks, three or four. On Sundays after church, we rode bikes as a family. We participated in life as fully as we could. We focused on what we could control—more laughter, more appreciation, more gratitude, and more hugs.

Because time together was critically important to us, I found faster and more efficient ways to cook so I could spend additional time with Dave and the girls. When preparing dinner, I often tripled a recipe, or created a few meals at once, to open up time in our schedule later in the week. I combined mowing the lawn with working out by placing Michelle in my backpack and carrying her around as I cut the grass. I prepared school lunches while overseeing the girls' homework. Even though the girls were young, we included them in helping with chores and handling their own laundry to provide more fun time for the whole family.

Dave, after a three-month break, returned to work. He was able to fulfill and enjoy participating in church responsibilities. He remained involved with the children's activities. By working and handling our investments, he kept up with our mounting medical bills. Most of the time, he felt and looked well. Every few months we made doctor visits. A variety of physicians took more scans and made sure his blood levels were in the normal range. He received all of my loving efforts to keep him well-nourished and optimistic, so he could retain a fighting spirit.

Dave's office sat right beside the kitchen, where I spent a significant amount of time cooking and cleaning. Michelle, still in preschool, toddled into her Daddy's office almost daily. Dave never shooed her away, no matter how many work deadlines he faced. She often climbed up the back of his chair and sat on top of his shoulders while he read through an array of papers layering his desk, or jotted down appointments in his planner. Sometimes she rested her head on Dave's full head of hair. Dave proceeded to work at his desk, take shoe orders, and make appointments. When she was more lively, Dave made up a game so she could remain with him when he would receive or needed to make a call. When he dialed the phone, he said FREEZE to Michelle. She knew FREEZE meant she needed to be as quiet and still as she could. After the call, Dave applauded her for doing a great job.

When Dave wasn't on a call, Michelle stuck barrettes, pink curlers, and bows in his hair. She adorned him with neon necklaces and clip-on earrings. Disney songs, often playing in the background, stimulated her imagination. She pulled on his ears like she was riding Dumbo. She squeezed his nose when she wanted the train to whistle. Every so often, Dave kissed her hands, arms, all the way up to her shoulder. Her legs hung loose, her toes wiggling in anticipation of Dave's next surprise squeezes.

A few months passed. The grapefruit-sized tumor sitting on top of Dave's adrenal glands pressed against his ribs. He managed to grin and bear the pain. He hid his discomfort from almost everyone, but not from me. I sensed everything he was thinking and feeling. We were dealing with this cancer together.

One weekend, the first of more to come, Dave remained in bed. The symptoms that had caused our initial concern had resurfaced. His heart raced. Pain flattened him. Sweat drenched his clothes. His worries about the medical bills increased. All this drained his energy levels. Dave's fighting spirit could not be extinguished. Even though he was physically and emotionally drained, he remained optimistic. He played John Denver on the stereo as he lay on the sofa. Sometimes he listened to his favorite songs; sometimes he sang along:

I want to live, I want to grow, I want to see, I want to know,
I want to share what I can give, I want to be, I want to live.

By Monday, Dave was back in his office. His dedication to provide for our family fueled him, even when he was exhausted. At times like that, I offered to help with his work. Together, we put shoes in sample bags, organized his folders, prepared and participated in garage sales to sell old sample Adidas shoes. There was never a time that we didn't look at each other and think, "How much longer do we have together?"

13
Always a Dad

*It's not about your mood and how you feel,
it is about your commitment to love.*
Lenny Kravitz

The week had arrived, and our family was excited to attend the production of *Charlotte's Web* at the elementary school. Sarah, a creative and happy third-grader, played the lead role. Dave and I had helped to paint the set. I sewed Sarah's costume and worked with her to memorize her lines. We were eager to attend the Friday afternoon event; especially Dave, who never missed our daughters' activities unless he was out of town on business.

But the Monday before the performance I called an ambulance and we rushed Dave to the hospital. A hormonal surge from the adrenal tumor caused his heart to speed up at such an alarming rate that we thought Dave was having a heart attack. Before Dave was diagnosed with cancer he had experienced similar episodes that doctors had not previously understood. The first warning signs had occurred when Dave was in Tampa on business. He woke up in the middle of the night, sweating and his heart racing. Not wanting to die in a hotel room, he ran outside. He was dizzy and nauseated. His head throbbed, and he threw up on the sidewalk. When he returned home the next day, we went to the emergency room. Doctors ordered labs. The results indicated nothing was wrong.

A few years later the same symptoms reappeared on yet another business trip. Physicians at a different hospital had come to the same conclusion—nothing was wrong. Shortly after the cancer diagnosis, our new doctors explained these episodes were significant and were a direct result of the tumor.

This time Dave was sent home with a prescription of beta blockers and orders to rest. While I had misgivings about his attending the performance later in the week, Dave did not. Friday morning, hours before the play, another surge of hormones from the adrenal tumor caused Dave's heart to race over 300 beats per minute. I was about ready to call the ambulance for the second time that week, but Dave slipped nitroglycerin under his tongue and his heartbeat resumed to normal. He definitely could not go. I knew that. But what about me? Should I support Sarah or stay home with Dave? Pale, sweating, and nauseated, Dave needed me. But then Sarah, my daughter, needed at least one of her parents to support her. Besides, earlier that week Sarah had fallen off the jungle gym at school and later complained that her leg hurt. Off to the emergency room we went again. The doctor informed us she had broken her leg. Determined to proceed with the show and despite the cast, she continued with rehearsals. I admired her perseverance. After saying a few prayers I came to the decision that I would go to the play.

I informed Dave of my decision, reminded him of the doctor's orders to rest, and emphasized the seriousness of his condition. He looked at me as if I hadn't said a word. "Dave, if you don't follow the doctor's orders, you could have a heart attack. I'll record every moment and you can watch the performance when I get back," I said. Again, a blank stare, as if he hadn't heard a word. He was bent on attending the performance. But I knew for the sake of his health that he had to stay home. I proposed having someone come stay with him.

64

He wouldn't have any of that.

After I prayed and asked Heavenly Father to calm Dave's heart and relieve his anguish, I gave Dave some medication to relieve the stress. When Dave settled down and was nearly asleep, I went downstairs and slipped his car keys into my purse to prevent him from attempting to drive over to the school. I rushed out the door and drove the golf cart up to the school, only half a mile up the street. Carrying Michelle on my hip, I maneuvered through the crowd of parents, grandparents, and dads racing in from work, to try and find a seat up front before they were all taken. Michelle, quiet and well-behaved, such a blessing at this time, deserved more of my attention. Surrounded by school friends, teachers, and restless children waiting to see their siblings perform, my mind drifted to Dave. Was he okay? Would he have another episode? What if he needed an ambulance again? As we took a seat, Michelle said, "Hungry Mama." I set down the camcorder and fumbled through my purse for some crackers. While she munched on those, I looked at the twenty-foot stage. Dave had drawn the entire Charlotte's Web backdrop—the Zuckerman's Famous Pig sign, County Fair in large letters over the set, the green pasture, mountains, brown fence, and barn. I struggled to focus on and appreciate each and every aspect of the backdrop. After a few moments, though, I could only see Dave at home in bed. He wanted to be here. I wanted him here.

We had the front office staff send Sarah a note that Dave wouldn't be attending because he had had another heart episode. I wondered how she had taken the news. When she peeked through the side curtain and spotted me, I was relieved that she looked both excited and anxious. I smiled and waved at her. She had practiced her lines for months and helped other children memorize their lines. Even though this was her first play, I knew she would do well.

Sarah looked toward the back of the room. Though her eyes filled with tears, she smiled. I looked back. There was Dave. Sweat drenched his white Adidas T-shirt. He walked with a limp and in obvious pain. Nothing was going to stop him from supporting his daughters. No key to drive, he walked, even though that very morning his heart raced to the point where he could have died. We glanced at each other. I can't believe you walked, I mouthed. Sandwiched between rows of people, unable to leave my seat, I couldn't get up to relieve Dave. He leaned against the wall and smiled as the play began.

In one scene, Sarah walked on the stage consoling Wilbur and said, "You have been my friend. That in itself is a tremendous thing. I wove my webs for you because I liked you. After all, what's a life anyway? We're born, we live a little while, we die." I contemplated the words, words that would leave a lasting impression on me. I looked back at Dave leaning against the wall, pride beaming from his eyes. What mattered most to him this very day was expressing his love for Sarah and demonstrating his support. Dave knew about living in the moment, and that doing so was worth more than life.

Dave remained during the entire performance. He cherished watching Sarah at her best—standing tall and acting her part with confidence and poise, whispering to others their lines when they hesitated or forgot. Though I wondered how he managed watching her through the excruciating bone pain and heart palpitations, I knew the answer. Love. Love and the desire to father his children while he could. His claps were the loudest. His focus complete.

After the play, I gathered my bag, camera, camcorder, and purse. I joined dozens of parents taking pictures, chit-chatting with each other, overjoyed with their child's performance. Though I was happy too, I felt an obligation to get Dave home.

How would I catch his attention in this crowd? Hiding his pain, he stood by the stage, the first one to congratulate Sarah and tell her how proud he was of her. How would I persuade him to leave? "Thank you, Daddy. Thank you for coming," Sarah responded with a smile, looking into Dave's blue eyes.

All of a sudden, I felt frantic. Where was she? Where was Michelle? What had I done? "Have you seen Michelle?" I asked a friend. "I don't know where she is." She smiled and pointed to my hip. There was Michelle. There was my baby. Stress had me in its grip. I was holding my own child and didn't even realize it.

14
Clear Answers

In the midst of our desperation, God delivers.
Dena Dyer

How could one word, two syllables, contain such uncertainty and confusion? I couldn't even say the word. It was foreign, distant, and cold. *Cancer* froze me with fear.

"I want my life back," I called out to my Heavenly Father as I was vacuuming one day.

"Are you still going to believe if things don't happen the way you think?" These were the words I heard.

I stopped vacuuming. I felt faint. "What do you mean?" I prayed. "I am doing everything right. This is going to turn out. Dave is going to live. Right?"

No answer.

I turned to Scripture that afternoon and in the days that followed. My prayer time became more focused. "Is he going to live? Is he going to win this battle?" I pleaded, desperate to have answers about our long-term future.

When I continued to bring these and more questions to prayer, all I heard in return was silence. Fear and doubt engulfed me. I wondered if God loved me. Or, had He forgotten me? Didn't he answer every prayer? "My God, my God why hast thou forsaken ME?" I cried.

As I searched the Scriptures, I realized there were better questions to explore. How much did I love God? Was I willing to lay down my life for him? Was I making room in my busy life for the Almighty?

Then I swung back from confidence to uncertainty. What if Dave didn't survive? But, no! We were going to survive this! He would survive! We would continue to enjoy our family life!

But, what if he didn't? Was I just hoping and imagining that he'd survive? What if the words that were spoken to me through the Spirit while I was cleaning were just my own thoughts? Was Dave really going to fulfill his God-given purpose in this life? Would cancer take him? What was our future, dear God? What was our future?

I received no answer. No tiny inkling of an answer. Nothing.

So I prayed. I fasted. I prayed some more. "I'm a big girl. I can take the answer," I pleaded with God. "I have to know. I just have to know."

If I told you, you wouldn't be able to enjoy him, was the clear and piercing answer I received, the Spirit speaking to my heart, whispering in my ears.

I was stunned. The tears flooded down my face. How can this be? Perhaps that answer was an imagining, one born out of fear.

Before bed that night, in desperation and in complete humility, I turned to the Scriptures. "Heavenly Father, please make your answer known in a more profound way. I don't want to doubt the truth. Please help me to understand," I asked in prayer. Then I opened up to scripture and read:

Blessed art thou for what thou has done; for thou has inquired of me, and behold, as often as thou has inquired thou has received instruction of my spirit. If it had not been so, thou wouldn't not have come to the place where thou art at this time. Behold, thou knowest that thou has inquired of me and I did enlighten thy mind; and now I tell thee these things that thou mayest know that thou has been enlightened by the spirit of truth.[1]

I then skipped around this page and these Scriptures stood out boldly:

Treasure up these words in thy heart. Be faithful and diligent in keeping the commandments of God, and I will encircle thee in the arms of my love. If you desire a further witness, cast your mind upon the night that you cried unto me in your heart that you might know concerning the truth of these things. Did I not speak peace to your mind concerning the matter? What great witness can you have than from God?[2]

That night I dreamed that Dave and I traveled to many places. Each place we went, Dave meandered behind me while I traveled at lightning speed. In one instance, I headed from our car in a Wal-Mart parking lot toward the store entrance. I was chatting with Dave about whether to buy something and wondered what he thought about that purchase. I felt frustrated because Dave was unable to walk at the same pace. I motioned my hand to him and said, "Come on. Let's walk together. Hurry."

In another instance, a perfect summer evening, Dave and I walked along a sandy beach that stretched across for miles. I inhaled the scent of the fresh salty sea breeze. I felt lulled by the sound of the water as it gently rolled onto the shore. I gazed at the pink and lavender sunset, God's gift to us. I reached for Dave's hand to pull him closer so he could see what I saw, something he often did when he was excited about a view and I was walking behind him. But, I couldn't grasp his hand.

Dave sensed my frustration in both of these instances. He remained behind me, resting his hand on my shoulder, offering a gentle pat as if to reassure me of his loving presence. His touched communicated a sense of calm confidence. In the dream, we were walking in two different worlds and communicating through an invisible realm. I felt a sense of incompleteness. I sensed that he could understand my thoughts, but I couldn't understand his. And then, I felt alone and devoid of purpose.

The clock read exactly 3 a.m. when I woke out of that dream. "Oh, Father, help me understand the meaning." As gentle as only a Father in Heaven could answer, I heard these tender words impressed upon my mind: "Dave is going to help you from behind the veil."

My heart began to race. My body felt cold. Within a few minutes, I was perspiring through the sheets. I struggled to accept these words. I turned toward Dave. I gazed at him, lying arm's length next to me. I wanted to share with him what I had heard and have him tell me that it was all in my head. But, I had come to discern the voice of the Lord through the years. I knew He had just confirmed the divine answers, not just once but three times. My whole body trembled. I slipped out from under the covers and tiptoed out of the room.

Downstairs, I collapsed onto the sofa in the music room and wept. Over the next six months, I continued to break down. I gazed at photographs of Dave and our family and saw Dave disappear or fade away. While engaged in my own tasks in the kitchen, I watched Dave work at his desk. I turned so he would not see tears fill my eyes. How could I live without him?

One day I drove down to the lake near our home. I sat in the car and sobbed. Who was I without Dave? He had helped define me. He had helped me overcome some insecurities and problems. He saw me for who I was and loved me—flaws and all. He believed in me. He cared for me more than I felt I was worth. I felt dependent on him. I didn't want to live without him. A part of me was dying. His love and life were what I knew.

As I sat there in the car feeling broken, I realized that what I had learned earlier in prayer—that by knowing the truth it would be hard to enjoy the time I had with Dave—was true. The answers and the dream were more than I could bear. I had asked and asked again. I had wanted to know. Now that I did, what was I to do with this knowledge? I wanted to freeze time, yet knew that I couldn't.

There in the car, I gazed out at the lake. I began to understand that the Lord was not going to calm this raging storm but *calm me* in the storm. Though I was looking at the serene waters of this lake, I saw myself floating on a small raft in the middle of the ocean. Huge waves collided over me. I held onto the raft. I slowed my breathing, just as I did giving birth to my daughters. I reached deep within for strength. I quieted my mind and prayed.

15
Fulfilling Promises

We don't remember days, we remember moments.
Cesare Pavese

Dave's office window faced into our backyard. When he worked from home making phone calls, he found pleasure in glancing up from his paperwork to watch our children on the swings or trampoline. One evening while dinner was cooking, I joined the girls for a game of kickball in the yard. I spotted Dave, chin cupped in his hand, gazing at us. He waved and smiled. His expression was telepathic. He seemed to be sentimentally yearning that the nostalgia of that moment would never end. I simultaneously wished that with him. Neither of us knew how much longer we'd have those special moments to cherish.

Ever meticulous with money, Dave made careful and deliberate decisions about our finances. A king of savings, he collected coupons and drove miles to save a few dollars. He spent little on himself, but was generous with others - especially the girls and me. He expressed gratitude and appreciation for gifts he received, but would often return them. He invested in family time and created positive, joyous memories through special activities and vacations.

During this time of wondering about our future and his longevity, Dave decided to fulfill the promise he had made to the girls about adding a four-legged member to the family. One

Friday night in October, after clearing the dinner dishes, Dave's circus-conductor voice echoed throughout the house. "Come one and come all! Come fast and gather around!" All four girls came running into the kitchen.

"The time has come! Something magical is about to happen. Your Daddy is about to keep his promise he made years ago. He is going to be true to his word! Tomorrow we are going to find us a DOG." The girls screamed, hollered, and high-fived!

"NOT a puppy! You can have a dog but not a puppy," I blurted out with a crooked smile. I envisioned the worst—the four-legged creature chewing on furniture, staining the carpet, barking at night, and providing me a brand new job—puppy guardian. No way! Dave looked at me and nodded.

Early the next morning, we ate breakfast and gathered in the family room. On our knees in prayer, we asked Heavenly Father to open the doors, guide our path, and help us find the perfect dog for our family. Then, off we headed to a nearby town to look at rescue dogs. All of the dogs were too large. We proceeded to a pet store. And then another pet store. The dogs were too big, too hairy, or too hyper. We entered yet another pet store. The girls were drawn to the puppies in the kennels. Megan pointed and asked the clerk to hold a sandy brown-haired female puppy with big brown eyes. The puppy, only six weeks old, began kissing Megan's cheeks, nose and chin, then tucked her nose into Megan's neck. Each of our girls held the puppy and experienced the same love. All eyes turned to me. "Not a puppy, girls," I managed. Sighing, Megan handed the puppy to me. The puppy sensed who was making the final decision and exaggerated its affection. Dave, wide-eyed and smiling, stood back and watched. I broke out into a grin. "How can I say no? She is so adorable," I announced.

"It's a done deal!" Dave blurted out.

The clerk, all smiles, shared that earlier that same morning someone had found that puppy in a box left in the middle of a parking lot. We paid for our new family member. Sophie was ours. She had found a loving home.

After Dave succeeded in realizing that promise of adding a furry member to our family, we also decided to plan some of our dream trips. We created a list of the top trips we wanted to take with each other and with our daughters, and the travels began. We took the family on several cruises and beach trips. Even though we had traveled to Disney World before, we penciled another trip onto the calendar. We began daydreaming about the famous Splash Mountain ride. Hopefully, Stephanie and Sarah would be tall enough so they could ride together. In the past, the girls were too short for that ride.

The week finally arrived and we traveled to Orlando. Long lines are part of the Disney experience and we waited in line for numerous rides! We inched along waiting to get into Splash Mountain. Unfortunately, Sarah was one and a half inches too short and didn't pass the height requirement. Dave, never short of ideas, went to the restroom and came back with a roll of toilet paper. Beneath a tree, he had Sarah take off her shoes and meticulously folded layer after layer of toilet paper until he was able to fill her shoes with enough tissues to increase her height by the one and a half inches required. "Dave, we really shouldn't do this. There are rules to follow," I whispered to him.

"She is going to ride this ride," Dave said, gazing at me with those tender blue-piercing eyes. "Work with me, Rachel."

I couldn't help but chuckle and hope for the best. Sarah moved stiffed-legged through the line like she was walking on stilts. She and Dave crossed their fingers. A different worker waved Sarah through after measuring her. Sarah and Stephanie held each other's hands and after they were well past the checkpoint, they gave each other a high-five and waved at us. We took several pictures of the moment. I can still see the sparkle in Dave's eyes. I can still hear the song: *Zip-A-Dee-Doo-Dah, Zip-A-Dee-A. My oh my, what a wonderful day! Plenty of sunshine heading my way. Zip-A-Dee-Doo-Dah, Zip-A-Dee-A.*

In 2000 Dave and I made a trip alone to New York City. We saw a few Broadway plays. Of the several shows we attended, *Les Miserables* was our favorite. Sitting near the front of the small theater, we felt a part of the play and found ourselves carried away by the love story and angelic voices, especially the songs, *On My Own* and *I Dreamed a Dream.* Holding Dave's hand, I felt blessed and grateful for having married him.

We toured other significant sites in New York. We visited the Statue of Liberty, and walked up the 354 stairs to the top. Standing in the crown of Lady Liberty, we looked out of the windows over the water and reflected on our freedoms, heritage, and history. Another day we rode the elevator up to the top of one of the Twin Towers, not realizing that a year later our country would suffer through the 9/11 attack and the very ground we walked would become a burial ground. That bitterly cold and windy February day, we walked out on the 110th floor to take pictures. We photographed the city below—Manhattan all a swirl with lights and people. We stood in awe. Dave turned to me and said, "Isn't it amazing how God knows all His children and is so completely aware of the details of everyone's life?"

As we rode down the elevator, we promised each other to keep the spotlight on the good times rather than the future unknowns. We would face forward and keep moving in full faith that God was guiding our lives, here on earth and in eternity.

16
Riding the Bull

The greatness of a man's power is the measure of his surrender.
William Booth

One October morning after days of spending too much time indoors dealing with a variety of responsibilities, I decided to take a walk through a nearby park. I find strength in nature— biking or hiking along a trail in the woods. The giant trees and stillness comforted me. I treasured feeling the unseen power of the wind and hearing the rustling of the leaves.

That morning I noticed a single leaf spinning in the wind without falling to the ground. I took a closer look and spotted a thirty-foot strand from a spider web that fell from a distant tree branch and angled downward to a wooden railing. The leaf, in the middle of this thread, spun in the wind and danced in the sunlight.

Enthralled, I heard and pondered these words from within, *"You can dance your best dance hanging by a thread."* Heavenly Father was impressing upon me that this trial was stretching me beyond anything I could have imagined. He was instructing me to stay close to him, to keep believing and trusting. Heavenly Father was molding me in His hands, as He was Dave. The way I responded to the pressure would determine the depth of my faithfulness and trust. Complete reliance on the Savior was the only way to face the challenges ahead. I had prayed for steadfastness. I continued to pray for the strength and courage to serve in the days ahead.

Standing there, pondering this shimmering and spinning leaf, I recalled C.S. Lewis' testimony. His mother had died of cancer when he was just a boy. Initially, he blamed God and became an atheist. Later, after deep search and *hanging by a thread*, he found meaning and felt the power of God's love and greater purpose. I also felt God's presence and power. I had prayed, sometimes crying through my own rocky resistance to life unfolding as it was. I had prayed and brought my questions, doubts, and fears about the unknown future to God. I was strengthening my faith through completely trusting in the Lord. As C.S. Lewis wrote, "You never know how much you believe anything, until its truth or falsehood becomes a matter of life and death to you." I needed the Savior and realized that He needed me. Trees have roots that grow deeper and stronger because of strong winds. My faith became strengthened and was continuing to grow.

As I stood there that cool autumn morning, a warm gust of wind blew and comforted me. When I went home I wrote this poem.

Warm Wind

Have you ever felt like a leaf
Twisted in the whirls of life,
Down to the ground below
Among the debris of mortal strife?

Have you ever looked up from below,
And wondered how God in all His wisdom
Could ever pull you from despair
And give you more… and then some?

At times have you felt all alone
Like no one cared
Cold cruel, lifeless world
Frozen, shivering scared?

Now look for a moment and listen
To the mighty rushing wind that warms
Beckoning hope amid the frost of life
Reaching then raising the form.

Peace is found in soul searching
For answers about who we are
What our destiny and mission is
And why we have come so far

The answers are found deep within us,
Search deep until you know
Then steady the course as day breaks
And go where the warm wind blows.

Several months later, I had a dream that became a tremendous spiritual anchor for me. I dreamed that Dave and I were driving through a rural area of a foreign country; perhaps it was Spain. We didn't know where we were or where we were going. We didn't have a map. We didn't speak the language of the inhabitants. We were almost out of gas. There, in that countryside, surrounded by fenced-in, open fields, wild bulls grazed on distant hills. We felt desperate. How, in this remote of an area, were we going to find a gas station? We turned down a dirt road, continuing our search. We needed a full tank of gas to make it back home.

After a while, we spotted *one* single gas tank in the middle of an open corral where farmers sat around chatting. I was relieved! Dave and I got out of the car. I walked over to look between the open slats in the wooden fence. Wild bulls grazed in the fields. I made eye contact with one black bull that looked mean and fierce. His head lowered. He stomped his right hoof. He took a deep breath and charged straight at me. My heart raced. I froze. Why would he charge at me? Why was he so full of anger? I am behind a fence. I am safe, right? I managed to put one hand out in front of me; the other hand stayed by my side. Only thirty feet away from me, a gate automatically swung wide open exactly where I stood fully exposed. The ravenous bull charged toward the fence. In an instant and in complete desperation, I threw both hands high in the air. Tears streamed down my face. "Lord, please save me," I begged. "Have mercy on me. I don't want to be destroyed."

The bull slowed his pace. Every movement he made was in slow motion. My heart returned to normal and I wasn't afraid. To my astonishment, the bull's countenance toward me instantly changed. I felt a sacred affection, a reverence toward this bull. This bull was transformed before my eyes into a gentle, tame, loving cow with the demeanor of a young calf. He approached me with compassion, confidence and adoration. Instantly, I felt exquisite joy and trust like nothing I had experienced before. The bull came close and nestled its velvety head into my neck. I saw my reflection in his loving and compassionate eyes. He saw through to my heart and I felt his infinite unconditional devotion and pure acceptance. I recognized those eyes as those of the Savior's. A deep and indescribable love penetrated my soul. A peaceful wave swept over me like warm water. *I can make this bitter thing become sweet to you, if you learn to get on the bull and ride it.*

The bull bowed its head, bent its legs, and lowered itself to the ground for me to easily climb onto its back. Once seated,he rose to a full standing position and turned us around to face a new direction. He moved with grace and confidence. Every step was deliberate and purposeful. The air was thin, and a warm breeze blew. I looked ahead toward the green pastures and distant fields. I wrapped my arms around the bull's strong neck and felt complete trust for the first time since Dave's diagnosis. I fully surrendered my will to His and held nothing back.

This symbolic dream comforted me. I became one with the Savior and felt strength surge through me. I kept my eyes focused on Him and followed his direction to survive the thing I feared most. He would deliver me from what I wanted for my life with my limited earthly view and lead me to a future of peace and abundance. Surrendering was not about giving up but allowing the Savior to teach, empower, and love me in a way that was unmatched by any other source.

17
Receiving Instructions

The one who obeys God's instruction for today,
will know His direction for tomorrow.
Lysa Terkeurst

I began to prepare myself for a future without Dave in this physical realm. I stopped asking God *when* and instead asked *when will I be spiritually ready?* At the same time, I continued to believe that we could prolong Dave's life through prayer, fasting, nutrition, and a positive attitude.

During this time, I made the decision to enroll in an online program at the College of Natural Health in Tulsa, Oklahoma. The innovative program taught both holistic and traditional perspectives. I absorbed the information on non-traditional therapies and treatments, especially those involving healing through nutrition. I read about a variety of ways to honor the body-mind connection, overcome fears, and to engage in the miraculous process of allowing the body to heal itself. Administrators of the college and instructors encouraged me to begin teaching while I learned in order to acquire experience. Fortunately, I was asked by church leaders in my community to teach members from nine congregations. This helped me more deeply integrate what I was learning and develop confidence in my teaching abilities.

Learning through an online learning community allowed me to fulfill my responsibilities of caring for Dave and the girls. My thirst for knowledge intensified and created a new challenge — keeping up with daily chores and getting enough sleep. I studied during the day while the children were at school and at night after they were in bed. I listened to audios in my car as I took the girls to and from their various activities. I read numerous books about prevention and how to help the body heal itself. I mailed in weekly exams and sent recorded interactive videos with my clients.

I took most of what I learned and put it into practice at home. I cooked food without destroying the living enzymes. I added nutrient-dense plants into our meals, sometimes even sneaking ingredients like spinach into desserts. I offered healthy snacks to the girls when they arrived home from school rather than cookies and milk. I surprised dinner guests with great meals made with fresh herbs and creative food combinations. I revamped main courses like lasagna and tacos into irresistible plant-based meals and shared these recipes with my clients while helping them learn to adapt their own favorite dishes.

During the next three and a half years that I worked on becoming a Nutritional Counselor and Naturopathic Doctor, I supported people to make positive shifts in their health through changes in their eating and lifestyle habits. A friend was informed by his doctor that he and his wife would never have children. Based on what I was learning, I put together a unique detox program that helped flood both their bodies with an alkaline diet, fresh juices, and consistent raw food through Juice Plus+. I also taught them to manage their stress through meditation, visualization, and deep breathing. Within six months they were pregnant and nine months later celebrated their healthy baby boy.

Another client suffered from irritable bowel syndrome, diabetes, high cholesterol, excess weight, and depression. After four months of helping her detox by making shifts in her diet and attitude, she received great lab results from her doctor: no diabetes, normal cholesterol levels, and the loss of twelve pounds. She reported having more energy and realized it was from whole food, rather than stimulants.

Stories like these energized and inspired me to support Dave to live as long as he could. I never shared with Dave that I had been forewarned through a dream that he was going to die. I believed that I needed to keep that knowledge to myself. I didn't want to squelch his hope. I also believed that if God wanted Dave to know, He would inform him at the right time. Still, I felt distraught, overwhelmed, and bitterly alone when I pondered the dream.

My walks outdoors in nature allowed me to connect with Heavenly Father and served as a reprieve from my busy schedule and more difficult emotions. Flowing creeks and towering pine trees surrounded the bike paths in our hometown. Nature seemed to talk to me, wave me on in encouragement. Sometimes, I walked for hours questioning, praying, and meditating. When fears of the unknown emerged, I stopped them by asking God to give me more faith. When fears of living life without Dave plagued me, I asked God to help me believe that I could manage the responsibilities of raising our daughters and managing our home and finances. When I cried or doubted, I imagined looking into the Savior's eyes. I heard these words: *Trust me. You are strong because of me. I will show you my power in this hard trial. You will come to know me better and look back on this experience as the most cherished and sacred time of your life.*

I tried to savor those words. My sole purpose became to know God and how He worked. This quest transformed my grief, doubts, and fears. Receiving instructions from Him became my aim. I began to experience true communion with a loving Father in Heaven, not as an abstract Being in a distant world, but as an intimate Companion who desired to communicate with me. He embraced and answered the questions of my heart: "Was this life really a preparation for the eternity? Was God really my Heavenly Father? Did He really love me as His daughter? Was the blood coursing through my veins filled with a mighty purpose from Him? Could I really draw on His power to strengthen and help me withstand the fiery darts of life and to someday return with honor to my heavenly home? Was what I sensed in prayer, what I understood Heavenly Father attempting to share with me, what I called 'my tutoring time' really coming from above?"

I prayed throughout each day and asked God to show me in detail how I could be a brighter example of faith for others to follow. I asked how He wanted me to help magnify His Love during Dave's illness. The impressions that came inspired me to begin preparing to do something that Heavenly Father had shown to me in a dream. That was to speak at Dave's funeral.

In the dream I stood at the front of the chapel. White fire beamed out of my mouth and into the hearts of those in the congregation who had come to honor Dave and what He had accomplished in his short life. This fire, this light, opened the hearts of many who were ready for His gospel. Angels surrounded all those in the room. As the wind blew, I felt God's Spirit in great abundance. I spoke without notes. God's strength held me up. Everyone in attendance knew without a doubt that the words I spoke came through me from God.

These were the visions etched clearly into my mind. The dream fueled my desire to represent the strength of the Savior and help others feel the Spirit in a way that they had not experienced before. I wanted to give back to Dave the greatest gift I could give of myself—to partner with Heavenly Father through the greatest sorrow I had known, to acquire the courage to trust in the Lord with all my heart and lean NOT on my own understanding. Instead of focusing on losing Dave, I began focusing on helping him graduate with honor. Isn't true love about allowing someone to progress and grow?

While growing up, my greatest fear was to speak in front of others. I didn't want the spotlight on me. In school I sat in the back row and avoided asking questions. When I was called upon, I froze. My knees went weak. My face turned red. I was so afraid to speak that if someone asked my name I wouldn't have been able to answer. My family and dearest friends believe in me. Through their belief in me, I began to speak in front of others, even though my heart pounded and my knees shook. I began to see my life in a new way and perceived that God was blowing up a balloon of confidence within me. I could stand up, speak out, and turn my focus from myself to others. God was aiding me to overcome inner challenges and insecurities by providing opportunities for me to develop new capacities.

Speaking at Dave's funeral the way I had seen in the dream would require courage and humility—complete surrender and absolute reliance on the power of God to work through me. While I wanted Dave as a lifelong companion, I knew that if it was God's will for Dave's life on this earth to end, it would be wrong for me to hold him back because I wanted him. God's will was the greatest path to happiness. And so I prayed that I would be given strength, wisdom, and peace. I turned my thoughts outward and began to consider how to honor Dave and show my deepest love to him by speaking at his funeral.

18
Task Master

Very often what God first helps us towards is not the virtue itself but just this power of trying over again.
C.S. Lewis

The doctors warned us that increased excitement and physical or mental stress could cause the tumor on Dave's adrenal gland to secrete too much epinephrine and norepinephrine into his bloodstream. This could cause an increase in blood pressure, heart, and respiratory rate. While many people are presumed to die of a heart attack, in reality some of them may die of adrenal cancer. Everyone's adrenal glands secrete these hormones into the bloodstream, but those, like Dave, with a tumor are at risk. The tumor causes significant health problems due to the excessive release of these hormones and resulting hormonal imbalances.

These warnings concerned me. I didn't want extra stress, even positive stress from the children wanting their Daddy to join them in play, to put Dave at risk for any of the side effects the doctors had mentioned. I didn't want him to end up bedridden. I didn't want him to live without his independence. Keeping the stress to a minimum became one of my new preoccupations. I took on the new role of protecting and guarding Dave. I became a kind of police officer at home.

Although my intentions were good, I began to sound like a broken record with the girls, especially when Dave's energy was low and they wanted to play. "Be careful! Don't jump on your daddy! No, don't ask Daddy, to jump on the trampoline. He's not feeling well today. He needs to rest now." The girls didn't like it. They could sense I was the gatekeeper between them and their dad, and that all too often I kept the gate closed by setting rules. They were too young to understand, too young to have the *inside scoop*. I could sense a wedge growing between the girls and me.

The wedge only increased in size as I also took on the role of enforcing piano practice. Dave and I had made the decision earlier on that our daughters would participate in one sport and take piano lessons. Stephanie loved piano and loved to sing. She never struggled with practicing the way Sarah and Megan did. While both Sarah and Megan had good voices, practicing to them was like a household chore they didn't want to do. I thought about scheduling in early morning practice before school and gave up on that idea within a few days. Mornings were just as busy as afternoons. Each child had to get out the door at different times, and I had to feed everyone. Dave was also a night owl and often slept in when I was getting the girls off to school. We tip-toed around and whispered. I hushed the children if they were too loud. I wanted Dave to get his rest.

Creating a practice schedule was challenging enough. Figuring out where to practice was another obstacle. The music room containing the grand piano was located adjacent to Dave's home office. I constantly shuffled the girls' practice times around when Dave worked from his home office, which was most of the time since he only traveled one week out of the month. When the phone rang or when he was making a call, I had to stop the piano practice so it was quiet. A typical thirty-minute practice stretched out much longer. I often bribed the girls to finish, which was ineffective. Our interactions resulted in frustration and tears.

One evening after dinner, while Dave was completing a report for work in his home office, I guided an unhappy Sarah to the piano."I hate piano," she yelled, as she sat down. "I don't even like this song."

"We'll break this song down. One measure at a time," I said, pointing to the piece.

"I hate piano. I hate it," Sarah repeated.

"We don't have a choice. You have lessons and you need to be ready," I said.

"No, I don't want to," Sarah persisted.

"Sarah, that's enough. Focus. You can do this," I insisted.

And we continued back and forth until Sarah broke down and cried out, "Daddy! Da-a-a-ddy! Daddy!" Her cries turned into sobs.

Dave came out of his office and stood in the doorway. He looked at me and shook his head. Normally, I would have persisted because I was the get-it-done, give-it-your-all type of person and wanted to instill that in the girls. Dave was the *softy*. The girls knew us well and tried to pit us against each other, creating a wedge. We didn't need any wedges at this time. We didn't need the stress either. Dave needed a healing environment. Piano practices and lessons were going to have to go, I realized. We needed a peaceful home. In that moment, I decided no more forcing piano practice, no more lessons, no more friction.

During this time, I was determined to simplify my schedule and focus on what was most important. Dinner meals were planned with purpose. We had a rule that we would sit down together for supper every night. We would connect as a family. Everyone would have the chance to share something that happened in their day. We would eat together even if this meant we had to eat earlier on busy days. In addition to eating together, I made a few other adjustments. Rather than doing most of the chores over the weekend, I had the girls help with one chore every day. This would allow our family to enjoy bike-riding, hiking, or picnicking on Saturday. I also volunteered less at the kid's school, church, and in the community. I tried to complete all my studies before the kids arrived home rather than cramming my homework in during the full and busy evening hours.

During this stressful time, we focused on what mattered most—family time. We strived to create a peaceful atmosphere in the home and more time together, realizing that our greatest blessings were love for God and each other.

19
Lost Ring

The value of consistent fervent prayer is not that He will hear us,
but that we will hear Him.
William McGill

One Saturday in April 2001, Dave arranged to have a large load of dirt delivered in preparation for our first real garden. Several men from our church showed up to help with shoveling the dirt since Dave's condition had deteriorated and his bones were not in the best condition. While the men worked, I selected and prepared everyone's clothes for a family portrait scheduled the following Monday and then snuck away for a short hour to have my nails manicured.

I arrived at the salon, took off my rings, selected a nail polish, and leaned back into the chair to relax. The hour zipped by and I hurried back home to Dave and our church volunteers. As I pulled in the driveway and put the car in park, I realized I wasn't wearing my wedding ring. I reached in my purse where I had put my rings while at the salon. They weren't there. I fingered through my entire purse. Nothing. No wedding ring. I raced into the house, dumped out the contents of my purse. Still nothing. No ring.

I drove back to the salon, only five minutes away, and searched the entire parking lot. Crying, I rushed into the salon. "Please help me. I've lost my wedding ring. My husband is sick with cancer. We've been married twenty years. This ring means everything to me," I pleaded.

The room was filled with women and men getting manicures and pedicures. They were more than eager to help. Everyone searched the shop. Ten minutes later, still looking, my cell phone rang. One of the men working in the garden called to say that Dave was trying to help out and fell. "Dave said he heard an explosive pop in his leg. We think it's broken. He's in severe pain. A lot of pain. He even screamed 'No--- No--- I can't die yet, I am not done!'"

I stood there shaking from head to toe. I had lost my wedding ring of twenty years. Dave had fallen. He knew that in his fragile condition a broken leg was not just a broken leg. He was so vulnerable that breaks and injuries could mean infection, surgery, pins, a speedy decline, and ultimate death.

Minutes later I was back home. We managed to help Dave into the house and situated him on the couch. He was trembling, sweaty, and dirty. I brought Dave some water. A neighbor who had heard Dave's blood curdling scream rushed to the scene and returned with some crutches to assist us as we went to the hospital. Before we left, I asked the men from our church to offer a prayer and request a healing blessing.

We arrived at the hospital well after dark. To everyone's surprise, the X-rays revealed no breaks or fractures. The doctor asked Dave to try to stand up. Dave hesitated. The pain he had felt prior to arriving at the hospital was excruciating. He took a breath and managed to walk a few steps. We left the hospital, Dave not needing the assistance of the crutches. We were overjoyed. Another miracle witnessed.

We arrived back home around 2:30 am. After Dave settled in bed, I couldn't sleep. I drove over to the parking lot with a flashlight. I walked up and down the parking lot. I couldn't believe that my ring had completely vanished. What was I going to do?

Back at home, I prayed. The entire next day, I prayed. The day after that, I prayed. On the third day, still unable to face Dave, still praying, I knew that he sensed something and sure enough, while sitting in the kitchen, he asked, "What's wrong?" I burst into tears and explained to him what had happened. Shocked, his eyebrows lifted, mouth parted and his face went pale. We talked about how we might find the ring and followed through with our plan. First, we returned to the parking lot and salon, yet again, retracing my steps. Then we returned back home to make a flyer. Dave drew a picture of the ring. I wrote out the description and our contact information. We made twenty copies, returned to the shopping plaza, talked with every store manager, and personally asked them to keep their eye out for the ring, offering a reward if found. Each manager posted the flyer and offered their support. Now we just had to wait for a phone call.

One week passed, then two. We received a few phone calls but the rings found by these callers were not mine. Three weeks passed. Then four. Feeling smaller than an ant, I could hardly face Dave.

One night as we drove back home from a school function, knowing how devastated I felt, Dave hugged me. "Our love isn't based on a wedding ring," he said.

I sighed.

"I'd like to buy you a ring," Dave continued.

"This will have to do," I said, holding up my hand. I had purchased a fake diamond already. "I don't deserve another ring."

"You do," Dave said. "You absolutely do. I love you. I want you to have another ring." He put his arm around me. I leaned into him, grateful for his love and understanding. We made plans to look for a ring with a beautiful stone that would remind us of our love, our lives shared, and our eternal commitment.

About two o'clock in the afternoon the next day, the phone rang. "I think I found your ring," a woman shared. She described the ring. "Yes, I believe I've found it," she said. My heart stopped. I felt the blood drain from my face. I arranged to meet the woman in the front of the K-Mart parking lot. Dave, sitting in the next room, asked who was on the phone and where I was racing off to. Afraid that this might be another false alarm, I told him that it was nothing important and that I was running out to the grocery store.

There in the K-Mart parking lot, I met the woman who indeed held a ring in her hand. It was my ring! She had found my ring. "Where did you find it?" I asked. She explained that about a month ago her husband and daughter stopped at the bank in this particular shopping center, the center where I had had my nails done. As her husband returned to the car, he spotted a gold ring glistening in the sun. He picked it up and handed it to his eighteen-year-old daughter, saying, "This must be a fake ring." Back home, the daughter set the ring on her dresser. The woman, her mother, found it there and knew it was not fake. The family began searching the newspaper, hoping to find a notice in the lost and found section. Even though they shopped at this plaza all month, they missed the flyers hanging in the windows of the stores. But that particular day as she walked into K-Mart, she spotted a flyer that she had passed several times that month. She had a hunch that the ring described on the flyer was the ring in her possession.

I returned home and rushed upstairs. I wanted to clean the ring before approaching Dave. I couldn't stop smiling. I pulled Megan into the bathroom and held out my hand, tears in my eyes. "Shhhh," I said. "I want to surprise your dad."

Downstairs, I tried to remain calm, but I could tell Dave sensed something was up. He walked up to me and put his arm around me, "So, where'd you go?"

"Nowhere in particular," I said, giggling, unable to hold in my joy.

He took a step back, looked at me from my head to my toes. Finally, he glanced down at my finger. By this time the girls had gathered around. Dave looked stunned. He dropped to his knees and kissed my ring. Then he jumped up, let out a joyful scream, and did a little dance right there in the kitchen. He hugged me so hard that it hurt. "Now don't you ever take that ring off again," he said and let out a laugh.

That was one happy day in our life, a day where Heavenly Father showed us yet again how he knew our desires, answered our prayers, and provided another miracle.

20
Hakuna Matata

Hope is putting faith to work when doubting would be easier.
Thomas S. Monson

One hot summer Saturday afternoon, Dave started feeling new pains in his hips, shoulder blades, and ribs. Exhausted, he wanted to be left alone. He lay in bed with the lights off and the blinds drawn shut. After giving him some pain pills so he could rest more comfortably, I explained to the girls that their daddy needed time to rest and that they could make all the noise they wanted outside, but not inside.

The girls had a great time riding their bikes, roller skating, and playing hopscotch in the driveway. They climbed their favorite backyard tree and read books in the tree house. They pumped higher and higher on the swings. After making a fort, they rode the golf cart over to the community lake, walked in the park, and later boasted about the turtles and beetles they spotted. What outside observer would know these precious children were also dealing with their Daddy's cancer?

Throughout the day I checked on Dave to make sure he had enough fluids and felt loved. I sat on the edge of the bed and asked him about the location of the pain so I could massage him. But the bone pain came from deep within. Massages did not help. I placed hot washcloths on the most painful spots. The heat treatment helped some. Placing my hands over him to apply what I was learning about the power of energy work made an even bigger difference. Prayer provided an even more noticeable improvement. Days like this proved that alternative methods worked more effectively than pain medication.

In between trying out these different alternatives, I ran downstairs to check on the children to make sure they were playing and not getting into any trouble. Though in excruciating pain, Dave was well aware of my efforts and distressed that he was unable to help with the children and household responsibilities.

Later that afternoon, he buried his head in the pillow. His mind filled with the old negative chatter. He was worried about certain Adidas accounts that needed attention, his responsibilities with the church, and house projects. He felt guilty for missing Megan's soccer game the past week and not being able to help with the girls' homework assignments. "I just want to die and get this over with. You deserve better. I'm tired, tired of watching you do all the work," he said.

Both Dave and I believed Satan worked to lower our spirits when we were most vulnerable and in physical or emotional pain. This was one such period. When Dave was working at home or away from home with Adidas, when he was playing with the children, he felt his life mattered and had meaning. His nature was mostly upbeat and positive. When he struggled to get out of bed, when pain overwhelmed him and strangled his mostly optimistic nature, I knew that he needed me to encourage him.

So that afternoon, I turned on some soft music. I shared how much I appreciated and believed in him. "You will get better, Dave. This is a temporary setback. Your life matters to us. Your life, in sickness and in health, matters," I said, stroking his hair.

Other days, prior to and after this difficult one, I set the children down at the kitchen table to write Dave letters of encouragement. Sometimes, even though in the same house, Dave and I wrote letters back and forth on the computer. We expressed our love, our thoughts, our gratitude, and even our frustrations. We found that it was sometimes easier to express ourselves through writing, even while in the same house.

After Dave relaxed enough to fall asleep, I went downstairs and cut up some apples, spooned peanut-butter into a bowl, and popped some popcorn. I called the girls in to wash up and get ready to watch one of our family favorite Disney movies, "Spirit." We gathered in the family room. "Can Daddy play horse?" Michelle asked. When we listened to the soundtrack to the movie, Dave usually galloped through the house like a horse and let Michelle ride on his back. Dave reared on all fours and jumped on the couch. He shook, stomped, and reared. Then all the girls wanted to ride on their daddy. I had many photographs of the fun.

"I'm sorry, Honey. Today your daddy doesn't feel well and he's resting. We have to be very quiet so he can sleep. We'll play horsey when he's feeling better," I explained. The girls accepted my explanation and gathered around the TV and the food.

During the movie, I spotted little Michelle, only four, leave the room. She cared deeply for her dad. Sensitive, she seemed to possess the ability to feel his pain, even at her young age. Her most beloved possession was a stuffed animal—a soft white kitty named Krystal. She carried Krystal to the park, to church, placed her in the car seat with her, and slept with her. She slipped out of the family room and tiptoed upstairs to our bedroom. She entered the dark room and crawled up on the king-sized bed. She pulled down the covers and slipped her precious Krystal beside Dave's back. As carefully and quietly as a four year old could, she climbed off the bed and attempted to slip out of the room and shut the door.

Dave felt the soft object pressed against his back. He pulled it toward him and, recognizing Krystal, said, "Michelle, come here Honey." Michelle walked over and stood in front of him. "Why are you giving me Krystal?"

Her eyes filled up with tiny tears. She titled her head, raised her shoulders and whispered, "Hakuna Matata."

"What did you say?"

"Hakuna Matata. No worries Daddy. No worries."

Dave pulled Michelle to him, and they embraced.

Michelle's sweet gesture was an answer to Dave's prayer and helped him press on and push ahead to enjoy more good days. Dave and I often marveled at how the Savior's tender mercies streamed through our daughters. Our daughters strengthened and buoyed him up through encouraging words and tender touches, through their innocence and love.

21
Isolation

Solitude is where one discovers one is not alone.
Marty Rubin

Dave remained active and continued to work when some of the metastasis in the bones reappeared. We continued to research experimental treatments to shrink the tumors to possibly combine with our non-traditional approach. Doctors explained surgery to de-bulk the main tumor was too risky and could only be done as a last resort. In 2002 we learned about a new therapy called MIBG radiation that could possibly minimize some of the recurring tumors. Not a cure, this approach might minimize the pain. We decided to give it a try, and because Dave's immune system was strong, the doctors approved him as a candidate for the treatment.

Dave took off several weeks from work and we scheduled a ten-day stay at the hospital that required complete isolation. This particular therapy involved injecting radioactive iodine into the body. The iodine would travel throughout the body and attach to the tumors, barely damaging healthy tissue. Our hope in choosing this kind of treatment was to reduce the tumors, control the periodic rise in rapid heart rate and high blood pressure, and reduce back pain. Prior to the treatment, we continued on with clean eating and tripled our nutritional protocol with Juice Plus+. We continued to pray and put our trust in God.

The day we checked Dave into the hospital, I walked up with him to help him get settled in his room. The room was completely covered in plastic from floor to ceiling. Plastic lined every stitch of the floor. The toilets, sink, and faucets were wrapped in plastic. All the utensils Dave would use to eat and drink were plastic—plastic plates, bowls, cups. We looked at each other and sighed. "I hope this works," I thought.

I helped Dave unpack. Even though we set up framed pictures of the girls and family, the room didn't lose that sterile feeling. We unpacked some John Denver CDs, the movie "Brave Heart," his Bible, and a journal. As we opened up the laptop, I wondered if Dave would even have the energy to work. The knot in my stomach grew. I tried to take a deep breath, but I felt dizzy, as if I was about to pass out.

The doctors and nurses emphasized the rules, strict as a prison's because of the nature of this procedure and the use of radiation. No visitors. No leaving the room. The nurses could only enter the room for a certain number of timed visits throughout the day. Food would be left by the door three times a day. Garbage was to remain in the room in tightly cinched bags.

"Time to get ready for the treatment," a nurse said, as she walked in Dave's new room. I knew that meant I needed to leave. I tried to hold in the tears and smile. This was our last embrace for an entire month. Even though he would return home in ten days, we had to wait until the radiation left his body before we could touch.

I squeezed Dave and offered a kiss. At the door, I turned to blow another kiss. When I shut the door behind me, I read the big letters written on the thick wooden door: DANGER, DO NOT ENTER, RADIOACTIVE.

Within a few hours, Dave called to let me know how he was doing and to relay what had occurred. The three physicians entered the room all suited up in what resembled astronaut suits that completely protected them from exposure. No skin showed through. They were able to examine Dave by wearing goggles. They rolled in a medium-sized gray refrigerator containing vials of high dose of liquid radiation that would be intravenously delivered into Dave. They reaffirmed that this was a safe procedure.

After injecting Dave with a therapeutic dose of radiation, one tiny drop touched one of the doctor's wrists where the plastic glove had moved and exposed some skin. He stormed out of the room. "I need to change immediately. I need to scrub down." All three doctors, panicked, cleaned up fast, rushed out of the door rolling the metal refrigerator with them. Dave said that his jaw dropped. I imagined him looking around the deserted room covered in plastic and gazing out the window to life beyond this procedure—the blue sky and swaying trees out the window, the framed pictures of the girls and our family.

Two days later, I was allowed a ten-minute visit. I wore a lead vest, a mask, and was draped from head to toe with plastic. I stood behind a three-foot partitioned wall about fifteen feet away from Dave. Short in stature, I managed to peer over the partition. Pale and tired but wearing his regular clothes, Dave sat up in the hospital bed. We looked at each other in silence for a few minutes, trying to hold back our emotions.

"How are you?" I finally asked.

"Nauseous. And I'd really like to go home."

"It's almost over. Soon you'll be home," I said, offering a smile. "I brought you some fruit and homemade soup. And I've got some mail for you and a few pictures of the girls." I tossed the mail, which included a letter I wrote to him. I updated him on activities at home. Dave managed to smile and proceeded to share what God was impressing on his heart—that the little things in life are the big things, and that all we can control is our own attitude. Here was my pale, tired, and radioactive-filled husband sharing spiritual insights. I was deeply moved.

"I love you," I said as I prepared to leave. "S'agapo," I added, which is Greek for *I love you*. "You are strong and brave. You will get better and be home soon. No worries. Hakuna Matata."

Ten days later, I picked up Dave. Though I was told not to touch him, I knew that was impossible and pointless. He was able to walk down the hallway and into the parking garage without assistance. Not being allowed to hold his hand felt strange. We received orders to avoid close proximity for several days. I helped Dave get in the car. Nauseated from the radiation, he leaned back into the seat and remained quiet as we drove home.

Back home, I helped Dave up to the bedroom, which I had lined with plastic per directions. While he tolerated the plastic in the room, the days of eating off of paper plates or using plastic utensils were over. He refused. The children were not allowed to come home for a few days until the radiation left his body, so they stayed with some friends. They came to play in the backyard, however, so Dave could see them from the bedroom window. I was to sleep downstairs and not touch him. I did my best but couldn't resist standing by our bedroom door, chatting with him, blowing a few kisses, and doing my best to encourage him. We prayed that the treatment would reduce the bone pain, shrink the tumor, and give him more time. We held on to hope and kept taking one baby step at a time. We chose not to think too far into the future. We were even more intentional about living in the moment and taking each day as it came.

22
The Letter

The more room you give yourself to express your true thoughts and feelings, the more room there is for wisdom and courage.
Marianne Williamson

One afternoon while Dave napped on the couch adjacent to his office, Megan, thirteen at the time, ran her fingers across the keyboard of Dave's computer. The screen lit up. Megan began reading a letter Dave had just written after receiving the news that he had about ninety days to live because the cancer had spread throughout his liver, a letter that he intended the girls and I would read after he died. Wide-eyed and curious, Megan began reading.

June 13, 2004

To my dearest family,

It's 2:15 am on June 13th. I can't sleep. I'm not sure if it's the pain, my rapid heart beats, anxiety, or depression over what the doctor shared with me this past Thursday, June 10th. He said I had about three months to live. Boy! I felt the same feelings I did when first diagnosed over seven years ago. NO, I thought emphatically. And then the slow realization settled in me. Everything moved in slow motion, like a cloud, a dense fog.

As I did seven years ago, I cried Thursday night. Hard. Real hard. I prayed. I begged to live, and pleaded with Heavenly Father to listen to the desire of my heart, the desire to be with you, my family, for many more years, to grow old with my wife, your mom, and travel like we've dreamed and talked about, to see you girls grow up to womanhood and celebrate your graduations, proms, dates, careers, marriages, the births of your children, and more.

I have full faith God will provide and protect, but I want to provide and protect as a husband and father. It's what I was born to do. I love being your mom's husband and your father, and I struggle to understand why this is being ripped from me in my prime. My heart can't take it at times. My very core hurts and aches when I think I'm not going to be there for you and you for me.

I'm 44 years old and realize I should be grateful to live the years I have, and I am grateful. I have lived in gratitude, but I desire to live to be 100. I know I'm not the only one who has so much to live for and has died young. But, the pain of leaving hurts like no other pain. When I see older folks together in a park, at church, or shopping together, I feel jealous. I see them and think how blessed and fortunate. In fact, I'm jealous of everyone left behind with a full life ahead of them because this world is so beautiful. I want to tell everyone I see to realize how blessed and fortunate they are to be alive. I want to shout out stop, notice and smell the flowers, listen to the water, and celebrate the variety of color and sounds this world has to offer!

Please realize that I'm not showing a lack of faith but sadness for having to leave this life that I love so much. Your mom is the most perfect wife. I will always love her as she has so fully loved me. We're soul mates. While it hurts to think of her with another, I know it would be best for her in time. That's all I care for – what's best for her. I know you dear children are resilient. You will move on without a problem. So many stories are told of those left without who excel beyond their peers. I pray that you, my dear daughters, are like those children. I want more than anything for you to move on with your lives and enjoy every facet of your precious days. I hope you will remember the times we celebrated life—noticing the very little details of the world around us, celebrating the sights, smells, and sounds. Remember the times we savored the taste of our food, ate slowly, and enjoyed the combinations of flavors. Life is so wonderful. Life is to be enjoyed. This is what I want for you after I'm gone.

Please do not sorrow too long after I'm gone. If you do, I will have failed in teaching you faith in God's plan and having gratitude and appreciation for all His creations in all its variety. Know and remember from my testimony that life continues after death. Death is an awakening, a birth into another realm of God's creations. I believe I will be close by, however. I hope you will feel me, when you need me most.

My passing will be one of your trials that you must conquer and overcome. Never get too depressed. Remember that death is part of life, and the sooner you're able to move on knowing God continues to watch over you and love you, the easier I will rest, and the sooner I will experience peace. I believe God will allow me near you at times. I will have the opportunity to watch you wherever you go from wherever I am.

More than anything, I want you all to know I believe the gospel of Jesus Christ with all of my whole heart and soul. It's given me the direction in my life that has led me to peace, fulfillment, and joy. I know of no other way to gain peace and calm than through obedience to the teachings of Christ. I am grateful for Christ and all he has done for me. He sacrificed his life for me that I may have Eternal life, and to that I will never be able to repay.

Today, Sunday, I forced myself to get up and go to church even though it was a struggle. I cried during the hymn "because I have been given much I too must give." I love that hymn. I am indeed grateful for the life I have had and the many fantastic memories. For a moment during that hymn, I sensed fully what Christ felt when He asked His Father, "If it be possible let this cup pass from me." He didn't want to suffer and be scourged, but he knew it was coming. He didn't want to die. This was part of his agony in the Garden, knowing that suffering and death were coming.

And so, the doctor has given me ninety days. I know death is coming. I, too, don't want it to happen. I'm afraid of the MIBG this time, the progression of the disease, the pain. I'm not ashamed to admit that for the first time ever, I'm afraid, and even nervous, because I feel like I'm dying and really think it is going to happen this time. Sometimes in the midst of all the pain, the anxiety, the sleepless nights, I think that death would be a welcome release.

I love you soooo much that at times when I think of being apart it hurts. I hated all my business trips away from home. The last few years all I wanted to do was to be with you, watch you study, play, and grow. I see so much light in your faces. You are all good girls. And you, Rachel, are the hardest working and most spiritual person I know. Stephanie, you have set a perfect example for your younger sisters. Sarah, you bring us laughter and joy. Megan, you bring us excitement and adventure. Michelle, you are an angel and the pure light of Christ for us all. You all mean the world to me, and I want to be here for you more than anything. I don't understand why this is happening and probably never will until on the other side. I hope you can make it through this trial and go on to have very successful, happy, and fulfilled lives like mine has been. I will be there in spirit wherever you go and a part of whatever you do. I hope you will feel my presence and remember the deep love and respect I have for all of you.

Love,
Daddy

After finishing the letter, Megan broke down. Whimpering she went to sit near Dave in the other room, where he was sleeping. He woke, sat up, and realized that she had read the letter "Awwww, Megan," he said, hugging her. "Let's go talk, Honey. Come on. Let's go outside."

Dave guided Megan to the back deck and sat on the porch swing. For over an hour, he discussed his love for her, the purpose of life, accepting trials, staying true to Heavenly Father and the Savior, and not giving up. He promised that he would always be close to her. He encouraged her to try and remain strong, even during the hard times. I remember watching from the window. Megan leaned against Dave's shoulders. He held her close to him. They sat together and watched the sun go down. Their love for each other is forever etched in my mind.

23
Unforgotten Prayer

You reach the greatest heights while on your knees.
David Burton

One night, feeling utterly alone, I wept from the depths of my being. Nothing could stop the weeping. What would I do without Dave? How would I handle raising the girls alone? Was I really ready? I couldn't answer any of those questions. The agony I felt was profound and immense.

I cried with the pillow over my mouth to avoid waking Dave. When the tears intensified, I slipped out of the room and made my way downstairs. I couldn't hold in the pain. I collapsed onto the sofa and sobbed into the pillow. Where was God? Did he not love me anymore? I felt like Alice from the movie Alice and Wonderland, so small, so insignificant, falling down, down into a dark pit. Grief consumed me. As I fell into the dark hole, I diminished in size. Had God distanced Himself from me? Had I fallen from His grace?

I began to weep. My own tears began to engulf me. When the salty water rose up to my neck, a thought reassured me. *You are not going to drown. My sorrow is helping you rise. Stand taller and reach higher for the One that loves you the most.* My sadness, grief, doubts, and fears prevented me from sensing God's presence. But even then, even throughout these difficult years, and now this most unbearable time, God in His love for me never moved. He was taking this tragedy and lifting me towards Him.

Several days later, I opened a church magazine to a scripture that connected to my experience. *And though the Lord gives you the bread of adversity, and the water of affliction, yet shall not thy teachers be removed into a corner anymore, but thine eyes shall see thy teachers.*[3]

Dave's diagnosis, this rare cancer, was our bread of adversity, our water of affliction. I felt weakened by this, sometimes betrayed, incapable of imagining living a future without him. But the Lord, my teacher, the Son of God was always there. When I was in darkness, He provided the means for me to see Him and be guided.

One Sunday morning, I did not want Dave to go to church. He was sweating and dealing with severe bone pain. He even had another heart episode. He disagreed with me, stating that he was planning to go. "No you are NOT going. You are not feeling well," I said, as I finished cleaning up from breakfast. He slowly walked upstairs. I heard the shower water turn on. I took a deep sigh. Dave had to do what he felt led to do. God was in charge, not me.

About thirty minutes later, Dave, wearing his Sunday best, made his way down the stairs, one step at a time, gripping the banister. Sweat poured from his pale face. "People depend on me. If I only have a limited time left, I want to give it all I have. People need to see me on the bad days, and if I can give anyone encouragement I will," he said and proceeded to walk out the door toward the car.

I stood there in silence. This was the man I married. He was strong. He was dedicated. He was determined. He walked in faith and with the utmost integrity. He demonstrated his faith through sickness and health. He influenced many.

Dave attended church that day. He stayed for a meeting after services. Those attending the meeting encouraged him to go home because he didn't look good. Dave did not comply. He remained in the back of the room leaning against the wall because the bone pain was so severe he could not sit. Some people asked me why he was doing this. I believed Dave had decided to live his life fully and completely until he couldn't. He was going to demonstrate his love for the Lord and our faith community until he couldn't. He was suffering. Yes. Dave knew the Lord suffered for our salvation. He was going to give his every breath to the Lord Jesus Christ until he physically couldn't.

Throughout the next six weeks, Dave's decline was rapid. I wanted to close my eyes rather than witness the love of my life, the king of comebacks, lose more weight, cringe in pain, slip into long bouts of sleep. The cancer had spread further to his liver and bones. Due to chronic nausea, he couldn't stand the smells when I cooked. How could I cook without creating smell? I had no idea. When I brought home food that Dave thought he could eat like cheese, crackers, cereal, or watermelon, he apologized and said he couldn't eat it.

Our neighbors and church family organized themselves to serve our family during this time, which helped me to keep up with taking care of Dave and all the household responsibilities. They brought in meals almost every day. They transported our children to their various activities. This helped me keep up with the yard work, the mounds of laundry, housecleaning, and paying the bills. Late at night, after our very full days, friends who had computer skills helped me with the computer and completing Stephanie's college applications before the deadline.

Many nights after the girls and Dave were asleep, supportive friends had returned home, and I had finished up some household chores, I found it difficult to unwind and get the rest I needed. My mind raced. How much more pain could Dave take? How much time did he have left? How would his actual passing occur? How would we deal with his absence? I tossed and turned in bed. I lay there listening to Dave's breathing, realizing that soon I wouldn't hear his breath.

One night after another exceptionally full day, I fell into bed exhausted. I pulled up the covers and realized I had forgotten to say my evening prayers. I rarely said my prayers in bed, but that night I could hardly move. "I'm so worn out," I thought to myself. "I was the first one up and I'm the last one to bed. I've been caring for everyone but me," I rationalized. Then I offered a much shorter prayer in my mind than usual and attempted to go to sleep.

About ten minutes later, I heard Dave turn to his side. He moaned. He struggled for breath. With great effort he pulled his legs around the edge of the bed and managed to sit up. Then he got out of bed and onto his knees. The room was dark except for a light from the hallway shining on his face. Sweat streamed down his face as he bowed his head in reverent silent prayer.

I had always prayed to see the face of God in my life. That night a reflection of the Savior came to mind as I watched Dave on his knees, his face tightening up with pain. I recalled the Biblical story of the Savior suffering in the Garden of Gethsemane where his sweat became like great drops of blood. In that state of agony, the Lord's response was to pray more earnestly.

After Dave struggled to get back under the covers, I lay for a while in communion with my Heavenly Father. He had allowed me to see a reflection of what the Lord had suffered through my own husband. He had answered my prayer. I saw the face of God in my lifetime through the man I loved and married.

That night I promised God that I would never again justify saying my prayers under my comfortable covers, not after seeing how Dave got to his knees, even though he had reason to remain in bed. He demonstrated his love for and faith in God until his final breaths.

III

24
Awakened

Death leaves a heartache that no one can heal,
love leaves a memory that no one can steal.
Unknown

Sarah

That last cold winter evening with our Dad, my sisters and I climbed onto Mom and Dad's king-sized bed. The cancer had spread to his bones, making it excruciating for him to walk. We took turns massaging his back, and Michelle tucked her favorite worn-out stuffed rabbit next to his pillow. Mom lit a small lamp, and we proceeded to read Scriptures and offer prayers. We took turns reading two verses each. When it was Michelle's turn, Mom helped her sound out the words.

After pondering the verses, Mom offered to say the prayer. Dad, usually the first one to get down on his knees, had no more physical strength left. He remained lying down. Mom, my sisters, and I bowed our heads. Mom began to pray. I closed my eyes. A few seconds later, I peeked at Dad whose eyes were closed. A frustrated expression and tears streaming down his cheeks saddened me. I wished I could make him happier.

Michelle was too young to understand what was happening. Stephanie and Megan, their eyes closed, looked sad. They sensed what was happening. My heart was also heavy, but I shrugged away those feelings. I did not want to face the harsh reality of Dad's passing.

When Mom finished praying, we all hugged each other and prepared for our special family handshake. We stood up, gathered around Dad and extended our right arms towards his. One by one, like we were members of a sports team preparing for an event, we took turns and placed our right hand on top of another family member's right hand. Our hands cupped, we then threw all of our hands up in the air at the same time as we simultaneously shouted, "Sure love ya!"

Around 5:30 the next morning, I sprung up into a sitting position. Why was I awake so early? I never woke up like this. And I never felt this alert so early in the morning.

Then I heard noise from downstairs. I hurried from my room to the end of the hall. I leaned over the banister. No lights were on. No one was there. I felt a tangible presence, as if people were hustling about and conversing.

"Who's there?" I called out.

No response.

"Hello?"

Silence again.

I shrugged and walked back to my bedroom. A light from my parent's room caught my attention. I opened the door. Dad lay there unconscious. Mom's eyes were filled with fear. I had never seen her so scared. She held her finger to his wrist. "His pulse and heart rate are beating out of control," she said. She rushed to the phone and managed to dial Dad's hospice nurse and asked her to hurry over.

I inched into the room. I remained a few feet away from the bed. Frozen with fear, I didn't blink once. I stared at my Dad. Where had he gone? It didn't seem like he was in his body. I put one hand over my chest, as if to silence my pounding heart. I felt so helpless. I stood there breathing, silent, watching my Dad whose own breathing became more labored. Mom moved around the bed and grasped Dad's hand. I slipped in closer to her and placed my right hand on her shoulder. I covered my mouth with my left hand, as if to hold in any sobs.

Tears welled up in Mom's eyes. She leaned towards Dad and whispered, "I love you, Dave. Thank you for showering me with love over the best twenty years of my life. You have given me more than I ever deserved. It's okay. You can go. I don't want you to suffer anymore. I can take care of our family now." With gentle tears flowing down Dad's cheeks, his face turned red. He took his last breath and died in Mom's arms.

In that moment, I witnessed and understood love like I never had before. Time stood still. A wonderful and powerful Spirit filled the room. This sensation was stronger than those clear and transforming moments at church or in prayer. I sensed angels there to usher Dad home to God. Mom and I hugged. I felt blessed that I had been awakened to witness Dad's transition from life to the other side.

25
The Viewing

With Christ, darkness cannot succeed.
Dieter Utchtdorf

Rachel

The paramedics covered Dave's body and wheeled him out of our home. Though my knees went week, I held onto our girls. We cried in each others' arms as we watched the ambulance drive off, the battle against cancer over. Though I could feel my heart breaking, I knew I had to keep going, to take the next breath, to move forward. Stephanie, Megan, Sarah, and Michelle looked at me with questioning eyes. I ushered the girls into the house and began making hard phone calls to family and the children's school.

In those early hours after Dave's passing, I reflected on the sacredness of my partnership with Heavenly Father. Six years ago, He had forewarned me of this day through visions and dreams. He provided guidance. He showed me His unconditional love in ways I had never imagined His love could be demonstrated. I had learned to completely rely on Him. When I trembled with fear, I visualized looking into His eyes. I imagined Him steadying and cupping my face in His strong hands. His words sunk deep into my heart. I had opened my entire being to His training in preparation for the big test of Dave's actual passing. I knew I must hold on tighter and believe more deeply to get through the days and months ahead.

Our church community, neighbors, friends, and other loved ones came to express their condolences, provide support, and take care of details without our even asking. They brought casseroles and flowers. They helped with dishes and laundry. They served in the silences as well, sensing just what our family needed. Another close and dearly-loved friend flew in all the way from California to provide transportation for family members who were flying in from out of town for the funeral. Two of my sisters were among those who flew in. Everyone's love calmed and helped me find solace amidst the sadness.

The viewing was held at the Carmichael Funeral home on Monday, January 9th. I had expressed the desire for a cozier atmosphere, rather than a cold and sterile one, typical of most funeral homes. I wanted the funeral home to feel like our own home. Two close friends went to work to make that happen. They replaced the pictures on the wall with pictures of the Savior and played the spiritual music that had comforted us the past several years. Rather than having Dave's body in a back room, they positioned the casket in the front and center where he belonged. When the girls and I walked in just before the viewing, the set-up was exactly as I had hoped.

I positioned myself right by Dave. Loved ones formed a line that circled around the room. The girls sat on a couch that we positioned at the end of the line. We greeted and comforted hundreds of people—teachers, principals, co-workers, family, and friends from near and far. After five non-stop hours, my jaw hurt from talking. The funeral director informed me that the viewing was the largest they had ever had.

We arrived back home at 9:30 pm. Exhausted, I took some Advil to relieve a migraine and went to bed. I felt like Jonah in the belly of the whale as I lay there with Scriptures in one hand and my notes in the other. I wanted to run and hide, even though I had thought about Dave's funeral since the doctors had given him only a few months to live. I had thought about Dave's funeral since I had the dream that Dave would support me from beyond the veil. I had thought about the next day for 365 days a year for over six years. I had practiced my testimony in front of the Lord thousands of times, always modifying to improve it, to honor Dave the way I wanted, to lead all those who loved Dave to appreciate our full and total reliance on Heavenly Father. I referred to those practice sessions as spiritual therapy with the Lord.

But suddenly fear flooded my every cell. All I wanted to do was run and hide. How would I ever get through the next day? I felt scared, as if jumping off a precipice. What if I fainted? What if I froze up and said nothing? I opened the Scriptures and read, *Fear not little flock do good... Look unto me in every thought; doubt not, fear not. . . doubt not, for it is the gift of God; and you shall hold it in your hands and do marvelous works; and no power shall be able to take it away out of your hands, for it IS the work of God.*[4]

I closed the Scriptures. I knew that I could not give the eulogy on my own. I had to rely on and trust in God to hold me up in the palm of His hands. I offered my heart. "Heavenly Father," I prayed, "If I use my notes tomorrow, I will not be showing true faith. I am fully surrendering. I am throwing myself at your feet. If I faint, you will have to pick me up. If my mind goes blank, you will have to put words in my mouth. I completely and fully trust you. I will do what you have asked. I will be what you want me to be."

After uttering this prayer, I felt some relief. There was no turning back, no hiding, no buckling under the pressure. I loved God so much and prayed that He would use me in my time of weakness to demonstrate His power. If I could help just one person witness that nothing is impossible to us if we have faith in the Savior, and that Heavenly Father lives and has a divine plan for His children, I would have fulfilled my deepest desires.

After helping the girls to bed, my sisters joined me. I turned off the light and pulled up the covers. We all lay side by side in the darkness holding hands in the king bed. I already missed Dave, but their presence helped me relax and eventually drift into a broken sleep.

26
Encircled with Love

*Strong faith in the Savior is submissively accepting
of His will and timing in our lives—
even if the outcome is not what we hoped for or wanted.*
David A Bednar

Rachel

Everyone stood as we entered the chapel, filled to capacity.
I led the way, the girls walking solemnly and bravely behind
me. The pallbearers, all wearing Adidas tennis shoes to honor
Dave, carried the casket covered with yellow roses, a symbol of
our life and time together. All eyes were on us, and tears flowed.
The girls sat down with family in the first row. Friends who
volunteered to record the service situated themselves. I took my
place on the speaker's stand and tried to relax.

The service began with the choir singing the opening hymn.
I pictured Dave and my Savior standing beside me. I kept my
heart on the Lord's promise. *There will I be also, for I will go before
your face. I will be on your right hand and on your left, and my Spirit
shall be in your hearts, and mine angels round about to bear you up.*[5]
I opened the program and saw my name. The moment had
arrived.

"It is an honor to stand here today. I look out at the hundreds
of people that have come—our community, church, family, and

dearest friends, and I want you to know I am speaking for a few reasons: because I love you, I love my Father in Heaven, and because Dave loved you.

I have never spoken at a funeral before, and I have attended very few. I have learned so much from each one of you. I would not be standing here today if it weren't for your strong prayers. I couldn't get through this day without you and the power of a loving Father in Heaven. He prepared and promised me that He would be right at my side.

Funerals are often a day of overwhelming sadness and grief because of the great loss in our lives, but I want this day to also be a day of gratitude. One of Dave's greatest gifts was how he lived in gratitude. I want you to feel gratitude for your relationships and all the blessings in your life. Look at the gifts God has given you. Think about the gifts you may not have but would like to develop. I want this day to be a day of reflection. Honoring a person's life at a funeral is a day to reflect on who we are and who we can be. We can raise the bar and strive to live a better life. We can make a more meaningful difference in this wonderful world.

Even though the trials of the past eight years were filled with pain, these difficulties helped our family appreciate the good times. Clouds hover over all of us. Challenges can alter our perception and thoughts. They can depress, frighten, and overwhelm us. Cancer hit and overwhelmed Dave. He found a way to look above this storm and through the Master lens. He believed he had a bigger purpose, and he learned to see his life the way God did. He possessed an eternal perspective and understood the grand vision.

In this world, it's easy to live it up, but to live a Christ-centered life, like Dave did, takes a lot of discipline and true devotion to God. In the front of the program, you will see Dave's favorite scripture. This scripture contains the ingredients for his success.

And now, my sons, remember, remember that it is upon the rock of our Redeemer, who is Christ, the Son of God, that ye must build your foundation; that when the devil shall send forth his mighty winds, yea, his shafts in the whirlwind, yea, when all his hail and his mighty storm shall beat upon you, it shall have no power over you to drag you down to the gulf of misery and endless wo, because of the rock upon which ye are built, which is a sure foundation, a foundation whereon if men build they cannot fall.[6]

When I met Dave, I thought he was gorgeous, but when cancer ravaged his body, I loved him more. I was so proud that this disease didn't crush his testimony. His roots were firmly planted in the soil of the Savior. As his body withered, his spirit soared. He radiated an eternal light from deep within. When pain consumed him, yes, he got depressed, but he didn't allow himself to stay in that emotional condition.

As I start this eulogy, I don't want to tell you about all the trophies, championships, accolades, titles, or positions Dave acquired in this life. They didn't mean a lot to Dave. He knew that what we take with us at the end are memories, knowledge, and qualities acquired during one's life.

Dave's life was extended for eight extra years because of your faith and prayers. Many of you, whole congregations of varying faiths, fasted and prayed for Dave. Thank you for allowing me that extra time to reflect on his life and on the beautiful person he was. My life has been forever changed because of him.

Dave lived every day with passion. He loved the outdoors and nature. He expressed joy for the beauty of God's creation and took delight in walking through fallen leaves, stopping to notice a butterfly sucking nectar from a flower, and hearing a bird sing its lullabies. He loved digging in the garden and the smell of freshly cut grass.

Dave noticed beauty in easier times and also in the most bitter of times. The day after he received the terminal diagnosis at the National Institute of Health, we were loading up the car and preparing for the two-and-a-half day journey back to Georgia. Dave walked over to a large oak tree, touched the trunk, and began examining the details of the bark. He had just learned the devastating news and had a sleepless night. Here he was, rubbing a tree trunk up and down. Curious, I asked him what he was doing. He gazed up at the towering oak and said, "This is the most beautiful tree I have ever seen." Dave had the capacity amid an earth-shattering nightmare to focus on the positive.

Dave was kind. I don't think he ever yelled. Kindness comes easily when others are kind. What if they are not? What if they are a bit different? What if they look strange or smell funny? What if they don't talk about the things you like to talk about or don't share the same perspectives?

A couple of years ago returning from upstate New York, Dave and I were racing to the boarding gate. Dave was about ten minutes ahead of me. When I arrived, I noticed that he was talking to a man as if he had known him for years. The man wore wrinkled clothing. His hair was greasy. He was untidy and rough around the edges. When the attendants called us to board the plane, I asked Dave who the man was. He grinned and explained that he had just met him. He treated someone he didn't really know the same way he treated friends, even me.

For Dave, it was just as easy to talk to someone who was just as easy not to talk to—someone different than himself, and someone that many people may have judged, perhaps even gossiped about. Dave hated gossip and never talked negatively about another person. This is true kindness.

Dave was energetic. Sometimes his energy tired me. Cheryl, Dave's sister, told me a story about Dave. One Christmas when Dave was about ten, he received a gift from his mother—fabric to make a bean bag chair. She had not had the time to finish making the chair. Dave whooped and hollered, cheered and hoorayed. When he finally quieted down, Dave's mom asked, "Do you know what it is?" Dave grew quiet, looked up in her eyes, and admitted, "No."

He was not only energetic but appreciative.

Dave also loved music and enjoyed singing. Gathering around the piano with his family as a child, and with his guitar with our girls, he loved to harmonize. When Dave was about ten, he had an experience that enabled him to make consistent choices about music. One day, Dave was listening to music that didn't sit well with his conscience. That night he had a dream that changed his life. Two people appeared to him. One pointed to him and said, "Do NOT listen to that kind of music. If you do, your life mission will be severely hampered."

Shortly after that dream, Dave fell in love with the lyrics of John Denver. He realized that music influences us in many ways. Music can encourage, improve, and elevate us. Music can also tear us down and cause us to give in to our passions. He followed the guidance he received in the dream and made choices about the kind of music he listened to that enabled him to live out his mission in Christ.

Dave, with his inquisitive mind, asked questions--many times the same question. He was a great communicator and knew how to get to know people in detail. He understood that the more questions you ask, the more the real answers surface. He liked to hear others talk about themselves and see them beam with excitement. One time while socializing with friends at our home, they asked Dave questions about himself. Dave turned the focus back on them. After our friends left, I asked Dave why he didn't answer their questions. Rather perturbed, he said, "Why would I want to talk about myself? I already know all about myself."

Dave's profession was in sales. For him, selling was not about encouraging people to buy Cover Girl cosmetics, Avia shoes, or even Adidas shoes. He loved people, and people loved him. He knew how to build lasting relationships. That is why he did so well.

What changed Dave's life more than anything else was when he served for the Church of Jesus Christ of Latter-day Saints as a full time missionary. He had saved his money and decided to give up his dream of a baseball career in the minor leagues. He knew that if he put the Lord first, everything would fall into place or fall out of his life. During his service, he saw lives change. Good people become better. Great people become even more devoted. Families were strengthened. Those who were missing God discovered the value of believing.

Dave taught me how to love unconditionally. I am lucky to have had twenty years loving and being loved by him. I would now like to end by giving you the greatest treasure and gift I have, the gift that means the most above all else, more than gold or diamonds or anything worldly. This gift is my belief.

Through the past eight years, I discovered that I could see better with my eyes closed, my arms folded, and my head bowed. Our loving Father lives. He loves us and has a plan that He created for each one of us. He wants us to be happy, and desires us to become perfect like Him. The Book of Matthew says, "Be ye therefore perfect even as your Father in Heaven is perfect."

Every time I try to be perfect, I fail. No matter how hard I try to work my way to heaven, I can't do it. Only through our Savior, Jesus Christ, is this possible. He can bridge the gap between our efforts and His power. It may take years, but through His grace, everything is possible.

I am grateful for how the Savior has carried me through this process. At times, he had to drag me. I love Him for not giving up on me. He helped me fight the raging bulls of depression. He helped me rise when I fell. Because of His atonement, we can be brought back into the presence of the Father, feel His love, and grow in understanding of His power and words.

I am grateful for the Holy Ghost, the Spirit that guides our lives. I can feel the Spirit here today. It almost has a sound. Can you hear it? Can you feel it? It is a reverence. It is a hush. The Spirit is strong and powerful. I am able to do what I am doing now because Heavenly Father promised me that He would be standing beside me, so I could get through this day. He told me that I needed to speak today and that He would give me the strength. I see fear all around me, but I am encircled in the arms of the Lord. You are watching me stand, shielded and protected, in the bubble of the Lord. I feel peace and warmth in this bubble, where otherwise I would collapse.

Most of my knowledge regarding our Father in Heaven comes from the Scriptures. I love the Scriptures. I love the Bible.

I love studying Moses, analyzing Samuel and Job. They all learned to recognize the voice of the Lord and act accordingly. I love studying the apostles in the New Testament, and their example of following Jesus Christ.

I testify to you that the Bible is the word of God. I also believe that just because He closed a record it doesn't mean He can't open another book. I testify to you that the Book of Mormon is another testament of Jesus Christ. It is also true. It solidifies the Bible's teachings and clarifies the teachings that are being misconstrued today. It contains the core doctrine of the plan of salvation, and it shows you how to find Christ and embrace Him. The Book of Mormon is a wonderful companion to the Bible. I hold them both as truth. Jesus loves people all over the world—in Jerusalem and in America. He appeared to the Americas after His resurrection.

Lastly, I want to leave you with two favorite Scriptures: From Proverbs, 'Trust in the Lord with all thine heart; and lean not unto thy own understanding. In all thy ways acknowledge him and he shall direct thy paths.'

From Moroni, 'Yea, come unto Christ, and be perfected in him, and deny yourselves of all ungodliness; and if ye shall deny yourselves of all ungodliness, and love God with all your might, mind and strength, then is his grace sufficient for you, that by his grace ye may be perfect in Christ; and if by the grace of God ye are perfect in Christ, ye can in nowise deny the power of God.'

I love all of you. This day has been made possible because of a loving God. I wanted to especially thank you and all the churches that joined our church to fast and pray for our family throughout the years. We have witnessed many miracles together. I say these things humbly in the sacred name of Jesus Christ. Amen."

I sat down overwhelmed and grateful to God. Throughout the eulogy, I felt the scripture *"I will encircle thee in the arms of my love"* come to life. Heavenly Father allowed me to speak for forty minutes without using any written notes, just like He had showed me in my dream. At that moment, I understood our true partnership and what being faithful and humble really meant. I understood the power and presence of God.

27
Look Up

Rachel

After the funeral services in Peachtree City, we flew Dave's casket and remains to Utah and held another large viewing and funeral service for our friends and family members there. The same invisible hand that kept me composed in Georgia carried me through the activities in Utah. Back home, however, I felt physically and emotionally depleted. I suffered from exhaustion, severe headaches and little, if any, appetite. I felt enormous grief that I was a widow and surprised that the clock still ticked and the world did not stop to mourn with me. I faced mounting pressures and responsibilities. I needed to help the girls get back into the rhythm of school, church, and extra-curricular activities. I had to sort through the piles of mail and medical bills. I had endless notices to read and documents to sign. The laundry didn't stop, nor did the need to prepare family meals.

One morning after I dropped off the girls at school, I returned home, closed the blinds, and crawled back in bed. I got under the covers and sobbed. I stayed in bed for hours until I heard a knock at the door. I didn't have the energy or inclination to respond. Startled to hear the door open downstairs, I sat up in bed. One of my dear friends called out my name. She had come over to return a house key. "I'm upstairs," I managed to say with a deep sigh. She came to the bedroom, encouraged me to get out of bed, and guided me downstairs. We sat in the family room, where I talked through some of my feelings. She sat by my side and accurately sensed that what I needed most was someone to listen, comfort, and simply BE there.

Numerous other friends and family members supported me in the weeks and months ahead. Even though my sisters and family lived in other states, they reached out to listen, love, and comfort me. They allowed me time to process the emotions I felt over the loss of Dave. They consoled me when I cried. They were patient. Their encouragement helped me to realize that tears are the greatest expression of love. To cry is human. To love and be loved are the most powerful gifts from God.

For the past eight years of Dave's illness, I had documented the hand of the Lord and His answers to my prayers in a small yellow notebook, which I kept hidden. I jotted down my impressions, dreams, and promptings of the spirit. I kept a chronicle of what our family was experiencing in bullet form. I suddenly felt an overwhelming desire to go through my notebook, expand on each of the bullet points, and write a more detailed account of how God had communicated with me. God had loved, guided, protected, and warned me throughout the past several years. Writing out more fully these sacred interactions would allow me to remember how present the Lord had been in my life. I didn't want to forget what the Savior had taught me. I knew my memory would fade with the passage of time. I eventually wanted to share my deepest and most sacred thoughts with my daughters, so they would know where to look for strength, answers, and healing. Possibly my journey could also lead others to understand the Source of divine guidance and healing.

And so I wrote. Writing and expanding on the thoughts in my little yellow notebook helped me to heal and focus on the good things in my life. Through my writing, I realized that life is an ongoing series of opportunities mixed with difficulties. Miracles don't always come the way we imagine. God had extended Dave's life far beyond what anyone thought. Despite all the emotional turmoil I felt since Dave's diagnosis through his death, God continued to draw me nearer to Him.

While writing and reflecting, I began tackling some of the items on my to-do list while the kids were at school. One of the items on the list was to purchase a glass top for our living room table. Measuring the correct size of the table was necessary to order the glass. On a cold wintry day, bundled up in my coat, I walked out to the garage to see if the tape measure was in the drawer with Dave's tools. It was not. I decided to check in the shed. As I began to walk toward the back of the garage to the shed, I felt Dave's presence – so powerful and real that I struggled to make it to the shed without collapsing. I missed him and longed for his touch. Slowly, I lifted the wooden latch to the shed and opened both doors. Dave's spirit continued to surround me. I bent over at the waist and cried out, "I know you are here! I know you are standing right beside me! I miss you!"

"Rachel, look up," Dave said. I could hear the words despite my sobs. On the shed's ceiling written with chalk in large white letters were the words, "Rachel—I love you forever! Love, Dave."

My mouth fell open. My tears stopped. I took in a deep breath. "I love you, too, Dave. I will love you forever," I whispered.

I sat on top of an old paint can and wept for joy in my sadness, realizing how close our loved ones are to us and that communication doesn't end with death.

Back in the house with tape measure in hand, I called one of Dave's best friends and asked if he knew about the love letter on the ceiling of the shed. "Dave wrote those words one week before he died. He wanted you to find it," he said.

I took a picture of Dave's message and tucked the photograph in the Scriptures to remind me of Dave's sweet gesture and as a reminder to LOOK UP in all types of situations. Dave knew that I would grieve his physical passing and that it was human to do so. He knew that I had learned to lean more fully on the Lord throughout his illness. He knew that I could and would survive his loss, and that the process of grieving would challenge and humble me. I would need to look up and remember the good times and to focus on the positive. I would need to look up to see God's fingerprints in my life. He also knew that it was my nature to serve, that I had the capacity to learn from the painful challenges that visit us in life, and that I would take what I learned and strive to inspire others to seek God for the solutions to their problems. Would it not be the greatest miracle if the Lord empowered me to transform my greatest sorrow into my greatest blessing? Would it not be the greatest miracle to look up and practice gratitude for all the blessings in life—the good and the bad?

28
Tattered and Worn

*The only person you should try to be better than is
the person you were yesterday.*
Unknown

A common practice in the South when entering a home is to remove shoes and leave them by the door. One day after visiting a friend for a few hours in her home, I went to retrieve my shoes near the front door and found *one* shoe. My friend and I searched throughout the house and discovered the other shoe under a chair. To my dismay, it was barely recognizable. My friend's dog had chewed up and shredded the shoe. When my friend asked me if I wanted the shoe back, I replied, "I guess someone wanted it more than I did." I left my shoe as a gift and went home barefoot.

Over the course of the next year following Dave's passing, I felt similar to how that shoe looked—tattered and worn. I was physically, emotionally, and spiritually spent. I had given all I had to extend Dave's life. For nearly two decades, I had partnered with the man I loved and now stood alone. Who was I? I began questioning my unique strengths and abilities. I felt lost, inadequate, and incomplete. How could life go on? I caught myself comparing my worst self to Dave's best self. I felt small and insignificant without him.

When Dave was alive, I enjoyed the privilege of raising our four daughters as a stay-at-home mom. Now, in my role as a single and only parent, I was struggling to fit into new shoes, bigger shoes, ones that were not as worn and tattered as I felt. Single parenting was demanding. I felt overwhelmed most days. I was chauffeur, chef, housekeeper, spiritual advisor, homework cheerleader, and tutor. I was household accountant, bill-payer, project manager, and exhausted. Stephanie, our oldest daughter, was preparing to leave for college within the year, and application and housing deadlines required extra late night hours. Each day brought additional surprise, worries, and pressure. I rose early in the morning and fell asleep later than planned most nights. My immediate family lived too far to help. Even though I had a large work and church support system, I didn't want to call on them since they had supported our family for eight long years.

On top of the busyness, grief trickled or flowed through every activity, depending upon the day. I felt as if I had been run over by a bus. I now had a new unwanted title: *widow*. Dave's *death* certificate and the word *deceased* brought on sleepless nights. I replayed the past. I worried about the future. I wanted to sleep away the days. I didn't. Instead I forced myself through the to-do list, frustrated and angry. Often, I lost my temper. I reprimanded the girls for not helping me enough and not being more responsible with the demands of school, church, and extra activities. I disliked making all the decisions alone. I battled with feelings of abandonment, rejection, and unworthiness. I wanted Dave. I wanted his love. I wanted his support. I wanted him to take care of me. I wanted a peaceful home. Many nights I fell into bed feeling like a total failure.

I eventually realized that in order to go forward, I needed to go backwards. In order to step into a better version of myself and rediscover my worthiness, I had to pause and reflect on my childhood. I grew up in a large family. I was the most shy and withdrawn of all eight siblings. When guests came to our home, I hid behind my mother's skirt. When asked to introduce myself, my heart raced and I perspired. When asked to speak in front of a small or large crowd in high school, my face turned red. I sat in the back of classrooms hoping the teachers would not see and call upon me.

Since Dave's passing, I had reverted back to my shy beginnings. I withdrew and felt insignificant. My self-esteem plummeted. Fear held me in its paralyzing grip. I felt guilty. For the past eight years I had supported Dave, I spent less time with our children. I couldn't get back that precious and irreplaceable time. There was only the present moment and the future. Though I felt inadequate, I prayed for strength. Even though I felt like I needed sympathy, I began to extend hugs and conversations to my daughters while managing the weight of the responsibilities that Dave had handled with such ease.

One particular early evening while preparing dinner, I asked the girls to turn off the TV and either get their homework done or tend to music practice. "Okay," they chimed. "Just a minute." The TV droned on. "Off now," I ordered. "Dinner will be ready in just a few minutes." There was no response. The TV remained on. I grabbed a sharp knife, headed outside to the cable box, and cut the cord. The TV would not control our lives. Our home was not going to be a home where that square box lured us into degradation and our lower appetites. My daughters were not going to numb their feelings of fear and sadness by watching one show after another. Dave and I had had a vision of how we wanted to raise our family. Even though he was not physically present, even though I was grieving and tired, I would not surrender our vision to my emotional condition. I needed a meaningful family life—purpose-filled with rich conversations and bonding time.

Before saying the blessing on the food, I asked the girls if they were mad that I had cut the cable cord. "No Mom, I am not mad. I'm glad you did that because now I don't have to decide," Megan answered.

Though each one of us was still grieving, though some of our conversations were not always unified or meaningful, this one act demonstrated to me the power I had to create a new and significant version of family life.

29

Coping & New Awareness

Believe in yourself and all that you are.
Know that there is something inside you
that is greater than any obstacle.
Christian D Larson

Rachel

Each daughter grieved in their own way after losing their father—a hero to them. My rational mind knew grieving was normal and an essential part of healing and moving forward. I supported each daughter by offering a listening ear, compassion, hugs, and connection. I didn't know how to handle Sarah's grief. Throughout the eight years of our family's journey through cancer, Sarah resisted talking about Dave's illness. Now that Dave was gone, she grew more withdrawn and disconnected. She began to pull away from me. Her affection towards me stopped. Her hugs felt robotic. She didn't make eye contact with me. I knew this was because she missed her father and the significant amount of love he had poured into her daily. Nonetheless, Sarah's withdrawal left me feeling unloved and insignificant.

I realized we both could benefit from seeking professional help to deal with our emotions. We needed to sort through unexpressed negative emotions and our grief. I especially worried that if Sarah continued to hold in these difficult emotions, future relationships with herself, friends, family, future husband, and even God could be impacted.

Sarah

I had simply never allowed myself to believe Dad was going to die. After an eight-year roller coaster ride hoping that Dad would live, I simply assumed he would. At the conscious level of thought, I knew he was physically growing weaker, but I somehow kept myself numb to avoid the harsh reality. I never went through the classic steps of mourning. I held in my emotions. I ignored the facts. I did not talk about what was happening. The pain was too overwhelming. I disconnected myself from the world around me as a form of denial and self-protection. As a young teenager, I was angry at the situation and did not know how to articulate or properly deal with my emotions.

I even began distancing myself from Mom. She responded by drawing closer. She wondered what was wrong, but that caused tension. I continued to take out my frustrations on her. I would raise my voice and roll my eyes at her. I missed Dad, and Mom was trying to fill his shoes, which annoyed me because her efforts did not feel genuine. Dad was naturally the affectionate one. I didn't feel awkward or rigid receiving hugs or kisses from him. Whenever Mom tried to be more touchy-feely like Dad and give me a hug, I robotically repaid the favor. Dad was also the better listener. Mom was too busy to focus. I could tell she wasn't really listening when I said something. She often asked me to repeat myself or responded with a delayed, "uh huh." Since I wasn't getting the parental attention I wanted, I thought "Why bother talking to Mom if she doesn't even care?" I felt like one of many projects on her checklist.

One time we were driving in the van and began to butt heads. She abruptly stopped the car and asked what was wrong. I felt stiff and hot inside. I couldn't talk to her about how I felt, nor did I want to. It would upset her. She then began sobbing and told me she felt so alone. So did I.

The following day while I was doing homework, Mom walked in my bedroom and said, "I've been thinking and praying, and I feel we both could really use some professional counseling to talk things out and try and mend our relationship. Would you be open to seeing a counselor with me?" I did not want to, but I consented.

Several days later, Mom and I drove to the counselor's office in silence. I had not dealt with my emotions before this. I had not talked to someone about them. "This is going to be very interesting," I thought to myself.

The counselor invited us to sit down. He seemed like a nice man, but I was sure even he could feel the negative energy and tension between Mom and me. He asked us why we wanted to meet with him. I kept my eyes on my shoes. I did not want to talk. Besides, this was all Mom's idea. After a long silence, Mom explained our situation, as she tried to hold back tears. I was hurting, too, but I did not show it. My heart felt heavy, but I maintained composure.

The counselor then turned to me and asked, "Sarah, what do you love about your father?" "Dad was amazing. He really cared about me. He took time to listen and understand. He was fun and made me laugh. He was not just my father but my best friend...."

"What do you love about your mother?"

Nothing came to mind. I thought long and hard. I felt sick inside. How could I not think of anything? There had to be something that I admired. My eyes remained focused on the ground. I could feel Mom looking at me. "My mom will never, never, never fill my father's shoes," I blurted out.

Rachel

A long pause caused my heart to sink. The silence felt like eternity "My mother will *never, never, never* fill my father's shoes," she said with absolute conviction.

I struggled to breathe. I wept. Sarah's words jabbed me in the heart.

"How do you feel about what Sarah said?" the counselor asked.

"I can understand how Sarah feels," I managed to answer through tears. "I feel the same way. I can't fill Dave's shoes. They are big shoes to fill. Through the eight years of his illness, he couldn't help but shower the girls with affection." I proceeded to explain that toward the end of his fight with cancer, Dave had allowed the girls to step away from responsibilities, provided numerous gifts, and unintentionally placed a wedge between the girls and me. He was providing excess attention because he was nearing the end. I understood that, and I would have done the same thing. Nonetheless, it was extremely difficult.

I felt like the elf doing all the behind-the-scenes work, in order to make sure Dave had plenty of quality time with our daughters. I did the work that no one noticed. I prepared meals and cleaned up the kitchen. I took care of the yard. I arranged for special family activities and trips for Dave and our daughters. I did all this because I wanted Dave's little reserve energy to go towards creating memories with our daughters.

The counselor then asked me to leave the room and wait out in the foyer. There, in the foyer, I wrestled with Sarah's perception of me and grappled with those stinging words: *You will never fill Dave's shoes.* Children will see what they see. I knew that. But, that realization didn't take away the pain. The tears flowed. Dave was gone and not able to comfort and console me. Sarah was distant and cold and in her own grief-stricken place.

It was then I felt Dave's presence. "One of the reasons why I had to leave," I could hear him say, "is so that you could come to fill your own shoes." I didn't want to hear those words. Filling my own shoes was beyond my comprehension.

Later that evening, I remained home alone while the girls went out to the movies, and I reached one of the lowest points of my life. Dave was gone. I felt inadequate. Who was I to raise our daughters alone? I didn't even know how to help Sarah through her grief. I couldn't replace Dave. He was gone. Our daughters' father was gone. What did it mean to fill my own shoes?

I couldn't stay inside. I decided to water the flowers out front. I held the hose and watered the flowers. I felt sad, worthless, and full of self-pity. I watched the water splash onto the petals, leaves, and dirt. I breathed in and out and calmed myself. The same words returned revised and full of possibility. The word *fill* deemphasized the word *never.* "You will never *fill* Dave's shoes, but you will come to *fill* your own and I will show you how."

I laughed. "You mean I can be myself and don't have to be anyone else, especially someone as great as Dave," I said out

155

loud. I felt like a new person and grateful for my loving Father in Heaven who nudged my spirit and lifted me.

That night, I came to believe that God spoke through Sarah when we saw the counselor, merely using her as an instrument to get my attention and help me become the person He wanted me to be. I wrote Sarah a therapeutic letter and laid it on her bed. It said, "You are right, I will *never, never, never* fill your father's shoes. I will come to *fill* my own, and you will have to love me for who I am."

The next morning I woke up early. My comfort zone was a peaceful place, but I knew that I could not grow staying there. It was time to get up, go out into the world, find my voice, and make a difference.

30
Yellow Roses

This is at the very heart of our sacred work –
to feel a spiritual impression and be willing to follow it.
Neil Anderson

Sarah

My eyes shot open. I sat up in bed. 5:40 a.m? How could that be? I never woke early.

"Sarah, you need to get yellow roses for your mother," I heard my dad say. His words were not audible. I did not hear them with my outer ears. My spirit heard them. I sensed Dad's presence. His spirit was speaking directly to mine. The clarity and power of his words startled and moved me. I got up, got dressed, and looked at the clock. I had just enough time to run the errand for Dad, present my mom the flowers, and make it for early morning seminary before school. Here it was, Mom and Dad's anniversary, the first anniversary Mom would observe alone. Dad wanted to make sure that she had the yellow roses she so loved.

As I drove to the nearby grocery store, I continued to sense my dad's presence. The veil between the physical and spiritual realms was thin. Even so, I wished he was actually sitting next to me in the car. "I miss you, Dad," I said aloud and began to cry.

In the store, I scanned the flower section looking for yellow roses. I saw red, orange, and pink ones. I saw yellow tulips. I saw carnations. I saw flowers I couldn't identify. "Dad, there are no yellow roses here," I said to him in my mind. I distinctly felt guided to move two sets of flowers to my right. There in the middle was a bouquet of yellow roses. My eyes filled with tears.

I returned home with the bouquet. As I entered the house, Mom looked confused. Wondering why I had left early, she thought that perhaps I went to work out at the gym before seminary. She looked at the flowers. With tears streaming down my face I handed her the yellow roses. "Dad woke me up," I explained. "He wanted you to have these. I didn't know it was your anniversary. It was his idea, not mine."

Mom lifted the bouquet to her face and inhaled the scent. She cried. I felt my dad standing by my side beaming with contentment. I will never forget this honor, to serve as an instrument, and run this errand. I felt comforted. My father was alive in spirit and still watching over our family. He was falling even more in love with Mom from beyond the veil.

31
True Beauty

But the Lord said unto Samuel, Look not on his countenance,
or on the height of his stature;
for the Lord seeth not as man seeth;
for man looketh on the outward appearance,
but the Lord looketh on the heart.[7]

In 2004 I traveled to Southern India to volunteer with an outreach program. The chance to perform volunteer work in a third-world country would provide my daughters and me a broader perspective, allow us to more fully develop virtues like empathy and gratitude, and to serve people who suffered.

We traveled with a friend on the board of directors with the Rising Star Outreach Program, a non-profit charity focused on eradicating leprosy and its stigma. We would help provide medical care to those afflicted with leprosy, assist the teachers in a new school that was aimed to educate and equip children currently living in a leper colony, and provide hope.

Stepping out of the airport was disorientating. The crowds and heat were overwhelming. The stench of garbage and urine shocked our senses. Cows roamed the streets, meandering all over, even onto the beaches. Cows mooed. Drivers honked their horns and sped around corners, weaved in and out of traffic, hollered at pedestrians in their way. People lay on the streets among the dirt and garbage, some ill, some begging, some whose eyes stared into a sort of nothingness, as flies circled around and landed on them. Most were homeless.

Gopi Sundaran, the director of the children's home, shared how he came to Rising Star School. He began serving by taking rice and beans out to the leper colonies in order to provide basic sustenance to those suffering there. This was only a temporary solution. He recognized the need to help people learn to provide for themselves.

I listened with awe and admiration. The spirit of God radiated from his whole being as he spoke. I was drawn to him and wanted to learn all I could about his deep compassion for others, and his commitment and devotion to God.

Gopi shared a dream in which an underground earthquake unleashed a series of killer waves that sped across the Indian Ocean. After that dream, he acted immediately. He boarded all fifty-three orphans on a bus and drove them an hour away. They were all spared. This dream and his swift response occurred prior to the greatest underground earthquake in history, the tsunami of 2004, that took 9,000 lives and leveled villages and devastated cities along the coast.

I had the privilege of attending Gopi's wedding and reception. Guests came from near and far for the special occasion. Friends, family members, and residents of the community attended. All fifty-three of his children participated. All wearing matching outfits, they sang and touched the hearts of everyone present.

I met one lady at the event who suffered from Von Recklinghausen's disease, a rare incurable and non-contagious genetic disorder that occurs in one out of every three thousand people. The disease affects the nervous system and causes tumors to form beneath the surface of the skin anywhere and at any time. No part of this woman's skin was spared. The tumors, all shapes and sizes, attacked every visible part of her body and completely covered her face.

I was taken aback, even shocked, by her appearance. What gave her strength to enter such a public place? I would have been tempted to stay behind closed doors, wear a mask, and avoid the whisperings and long stares. Friends surrounded her. She interacted and communicated with them in a caring way. She walked with poise and elegance. I witnessed in her the marks of profound courage, confidence, and beauty. She possessed a zest for life. Despite the tumors, scars, and deformity, she radiated inner beauty. Elizabeth Kubler-Ross said, "True beauty is revealed only if there is a light from within."

Who was this amazing woman? I stood back and watched her from a distance, as she walked down the reception hall to stand in the reception line to congratulate Gopi and his lovely bride. I wondered how Gopi knew her and if I might tell the depth of their relationship by their greeting.

Gopi shook hands, smiled, and chatted with the guests in the reception line. When the woman approached him, he focused all his attention on her, smiled, and called her by name. He did not let others rush or distract him. He embraced her, held her face with both hands, and kissed her on the forehead. Their affection for each other was as obvious as the abnormality that had overtaken every part of her outward appearance.

In that moment, I saw beauty and caught a glimpse of the Savior's love for all people. This was how the Savior would embrace, greet, and kiss me, if I were standing in that wedding line. He would not focus on my numerous imperfections but on the beauty found within my being.

After two transforming weeks in India, my daughters and I left the country filled with gratitude. What we remember most were the lessons of selfless service and lasting friendship. We met people who could not hide behind masks, wealth, and pretty clothes. We met people who were poor in material possessions, and many who suffered from disorders and diseases. These people were rich in their hearts and faith. They lived authentically and gave of themselves.

32

Desperate in Deep Waters

When a man has no strength, if he leans on God,
he becomes powerful.
Dwight Lyman Moody

I was pleased when Sarah, in her early twenties, decided to spend eighteen months serving a church mission. She sent weekly letters, which bridged the thousands of miles between us. The letters revealed significant spiritual growth. She was drawing closer to God and becoming articulate about matters of the heart.

In one letter, she shared how she had successive conversations with a particular gentleman. In their first conversation, she asked the man who Jesus Christ was to him. "A man in history," he responded, dismissively. Several lessons later, Sarah asked the same question. "Jesus was born in Bethlehem. He performed many miracles. He taught people to love deeply and sacrifice much," he answered. Time passed. Sarah asked the gentleman the same question. "He is my Savior," the man answered, bowing his head in tears. The man was baptized the next day.

Stories like these renewed my own love for the Savior. I pondered the role Jesus played in my life. I pleaded with my Father in Heaven to increase my love for Jesus, to deepen my devotions, to increase the role of the Lord in my life.

One particularly hot summer night a few months later, I decided to start training for the swimming portion of an upcoming triathlon. I drove to the Peachtree City Lake to practice the 1.2 mile swim. Could I manage the distance without struggling? Was I in good enough shape? I couldn't remember when I had last swum such a distance without being able to touch and stand at the bottom of a lake or pool to rest. I was nervous.

As I walked down to the lake, I felt the red Georgia clay between my toes. Tiny bugs skimmed across the water. I spotted six or so swimmers at practice, coming and going in different directions. I would have preferred swimming in a clear, refreshing pool, but I plunged into the water and decided to ignore what was lurking beneath the surface.

I managed the first half of the swim and then hit a wall of fatigue. My breathing grew inconsistent. I mixed in breaststrokes, backstrokes, and sidestrokes to give myself a break from freestyle strokes. Exhaustion replaced fatigue. I began to panic. I couldn't turn back. I couldn't touch the bottom to rest. My sloppy strokes weren't moving me forward. I tried to relax and talk myself out of the anxiety I was feeling. *Focus. One stroke at a time. Relax. Preserve your energy. You can do this.* My words seemed to fall on deaf ears. *God, I can't do this. I need Your help. Get me back to shore. Safely. I want to live. I don't want to die young. Help.*

I glanced over to my right. A short distance from me, I spotted a man. Was he struggling? Was he trying to stay afloat? Was I imagining this? I cleared the water from my eyes. There was, in fact, a man bobbing up and down in the water. Exhausted, I worried that if I tried to save him, he might pull me under, and we both would drown. I was frightened, out of breath, and had little strength. For a moment, I imagined my children being orphans.

That imagining caused me to push through my frozen panic in a split-second. As if a higher source had taken control, I had what felt like an out-of-body experience. I swam over to the man. "Relax," I said, completely out of breath, "Just float on your back and take my hand." He told me he couldn't see anything. His glassy eyes didn't blink. I wondered if he had had a stroke. Grasping his arm, and with more strength than I knew I could ever possess, I turned my face up to the sky, squinted, and breathed like the world was running out of air.

Adrenaline rushed through my body. An invisible hand provided energy and strength. I felt safe and uneasy at the same time. I yelled out to another swimmer to come assist me. He swam over to help. Finally, we were able to touch the bottom of the lake, stand, and bring the man to shore. We called the paramedics. They arrived within minutes and rushed him to the hospital.

I sat on shore somewhat dazed, perhaps even in a state of shock, and rested for a while. Then I proceeded to finish my workout and return to where I had started. Back in the water, I swam and replayed what had occurred. The outcome could have been different. What if I had not seen the man in crisis or lacked the courage to help? Would the Lord have seen a refusal to help as an affront? My floundering in the lake was no coincidence, I realized. Anxiousness overcame me and positioned me in the very spot I was needed to save a life. I had always believed that the Lord could provide the help we needed through another person. In this case, I was that other person.

As I continued swimming and pondering, I grew tired. Where was the shoreline? I had had enough swimming for one day. I focused on taking longer, smoother strokes. *"Look unto me in every thought, doubt not, fear not. My arm is over all the earth and my hands are stretched out still."* Every now and then, I looked up to see if I was getting closer. Finally, I reached shore and walked out of the water. My hands and body were tired. My heart was full. The Savior had used me to save a life.

Two days later, I received a phone call from the man who had nearly drowned. Arnold thanked me and shared his recollections. Halfway out in the lake, he found himself struggling to breathe. He began to float to catch his breath. He could not keep himself above water. He sank, went to the bottom of the lake, and pushed himself back up to the surface. This happened a second time and a third. "If no one helps me when I surface this last time, I'm going to drown," he thought to himself. That was when I had realized he was in trouble and swam over to help him. He was grateful that we called an ambulance and shared that the doctors believed he had a blood clot in his lungs.

After talking to Arnold I felt profound gratitude that I had served as an instrument in taking someone through the darkness to the break of one more day. Heavenly Father demonstrated His power, matchless love, and saving grace. He reached out to save us both.

"Who is Jesus to you?" Sarah had posed to the gentleman she had met on her mission trip. Now I wondered, who was Jesus to me? Despite our weakness in the water, the Savior rescued Arnold and me with His powerful outstretched hands. Even if we were in murky waters, over our heads in problems, and struggling to make it through the day, the Lord made bare His holy arms and came swiftly to our aid. Jesus was my Savior, Redeemer, Elder Brother, and personal friend. He was my Master. He was the All-Mighty.

33
Core Calling

Death isn't the greatest loss.
The greatest loss is what you let die
when you are still alive.
Norman Cousins

After Dave's passing, I felt overwhelmed by all the responsibilities that Dave and I had shared. My children looked to me. I was now the head of the household. My daughters needed me to be confident and capable, yet I felt inadequate. I didn't know how to handle family life, household management, maintenance, and finances, all on my own. I needed to build my business, yet I had never run a business before. I collapsed into bed at night, exhausted and frustrated. I didn't get to half of what I had planned to accomplish. Crying, I reached for Dave across the empty bed. I wanted him there. I wanted my life back.

I woke up determined to make each day better than the one before. I prayed. I asked for God's help. I realized that I had to let go of trying to manage everything myself, and that I needed help. Three of my favorite words became: do, delegate, delete. I tackled my never-ending lists by deciding what could be delegated or deleted. That streamlined the to-do list. I hired a bookkeeper, lawn care services, and asked for help to accomplish several other chores. I came to understand not everything has to be done. I made conscientious decisions about what I could do.

I also committed to making personal changes. "You will never, never, never fill Dave's shoes," Sarah had said. I told Sarah that I would not even try to fill her father's shoes. Instead, I would fill my own. To do that, I had to stop wishing things were different. I had to create my life. I needed medical insurance for my children and a flexible schedule to work around their activities. I needed something to fuel my spirit, bring fulfillment, and help me progress.

One morning while praying for solutions, I glanced at my bookshelf. *Today Matters*, a book by John Maxwell, a writer on personal and business development, stood out. My life mattered. I needed to seize the day. My work as a naturopath and my involvement with the Juice Plus+ Company were meaningful, fulfilling, and provided possibilities. *Get up and seize the day. Take action. If it's going to be, it's up to me.* I needed to focus and to ask for guidance. I reached out to a top business partner at Juice Plus+ and asked for help to create a game plan to reach the top leadership position, so that I could receive full benefits, which included a comprehensive health package and college tuition support.

In an instant I knew what to do. After Dave's diagnosis and witnessing the power of food to prolong life, I had earned a dual degree as Nutritional Counselor and Naturopathic Doctor. I had begun working on a part-time basis during Dave's illness, counseling clients on making health and lifestyle changes. I had also started a franchise with the Juice Plus+ Company to help them add more whole foods into their diets. My clients struggled to meet the daily requirement of fruits and vegetables and were eager to add a convenient and affordable way to get a wider variety of plants to reduce their risk for disease.

I was now ready to take myself seriously and work as a full-time professional. I had a powerful story of how faith, prayer, fasting, and whole foods had extended the life of my husband. God was calling me to step out of my comfort zone, transform my life, and to offer others my services. Heavenly Father was turning my deepest wound into my core calling.

Even on days when I continued to struggle with feelings of grief, I showed up and conducted business. By doing so, I learned that taking action is the most effective way to change my mood. I began to more thoroughly develop my skills. I set goals, created a daily method of operation, tracked my progress, and held myself accountable. As a result, I acquired new customers and new business partners, who shared the passion of inspiring healthy living through whole food nutrition. I conducted wellness events of all sizes. I facilitated mastermind and training sessions to create business strategies. I eliminated self-defeating thoughts. If I didn't know how to do something, I did it anyway, trusting the process. I remained on the path to leadership.

I turned my attention from my challenges to helping others make progress. I taught others how the body creates its own internal pharmacy through exercise, proper nutrition, and other pillars of health. Clients and customers returned with their healing stories. Some no longer needed medication. Many dropped unnecessary pounds. Those struggling with insomnia slept better. Moms were thrilled that their kids were consuming the kinds of fruits and vegetables that they had shunned in the past. After a couple of months one child, a junk food-aholic, shared that his "candy" didn't taste the same and that he didn't like it anymore. Because of the raw food he ate, because his body was getting what it needed, he experienced what many doctors refer to as metabolic reprogramming and he began desiring healthier food. I celebrated with my clients and customers. We marveled at how the body could heal itself with the right nutrition.

Personal development was a critical part of my growing my business. Dave had modeled to me exemplary communication skills and confidence. He oozed with personality. I perceived myself as shy, and lacking in confidence and personality. I could change. Because of my determination to grow, I filled and read an entire bookshelf on personal growth and communication. I attended seminars. I listened to recordings. I learned new concepts and applied them. When I shared with my daughters that I was reading a book titled, *How to Talk to Anyone*, my oldest laughed. That didn't stop me from teaching them what I was learning and having them join in on practicing important life skills. Once a month I invited a few families for dinner to practice connecting with people and appreciating them. My daughters joined in. Our mission was to create the best time of our guests' lives at our home by asking great questions to learn about them and NOT talking about ourselves. The questions were designed to include everyone at the table. I turned our social gatherings into a game of making others feel good. Our family began creating some new and deep friendships. We grew closer together as well, and deep inner healing occurred. Connecting with and making others feel important and valued helped us overcome our sadness and grief.

I set my intention to become a National Marketing Director. To reach this goal in two years, I needed the support of my daughters. I explained to them that I needed their help with household chores. When I was on the phone with customers and clients, I also needed them to cooperate by not interrupting or complaining. When I reached the big promotion, I promised them that we would all celebrate at Disney World. When they complained while I was on the phone or working, I smiled and said, "Disney," offering a thumbs up. This reminder worked. The complaints decreased. We worked together as a team.

Instead of complaining and worrying about my weaknesses, I focused on my strengths and gifts. I spent time with positive people. "You gain strength, courage, and confidence by every experience in which you really stop to look fear in the face. You must do the thing which you think you cannot do." Sayings like this from Eleanor Roosevelt inspired me to do what I had never done, to step where I had not gone before.

I forced myself to join a local networking group as a way to meet new people and overcome my shyness. I can still remember the first time I introduced myself to twenty local business professionals. My heart pounded. My face turned red. My voice trembled. I went home with a splitting headache. This didn't stop me. I knew that the only way to grow was to move through my fears, not away from or around them. I forced myself to return the following week.

Two years after Dave passed away, I received the phone call from the Juice Plus Company. My mentors in the field and at the corporate office were all on the phone. They congratulated me. I had met the requirements to reach the top position. I sat down on a chair in the kitchen and wept for joy. Then I knelt down and thanked my Heavenly Father for giving our family strength to do the impossible. When my daughters returned from school, I shared the news. We hugged, screamed, and cried tears of joy. We then offered prayers of gratitude for God's direction and guidance.

I found my voice by taking to heart the words, "You will never *fill* Dave's shoes but you will *fill* your own and I will show you how." These words were a message to me from God. Sarah had been an instrument to convey them. Though we both went through challenges and pain, and our relationship appeared to be fragile after Dave's passing, we both came to see how God transformed our limited perceptions of one another.

171

I began to *fill* my own shoes. I began to love myself and stop destructive patterns of self-criticism. I learned to embrace mistakes and learn from them. I focused on making personal progress, rather than making unhealthy comparisons or engaging in unhealthy competition. I let go of complacency. I made a commitment to be the *best* version of myself every day. I allowed myself to receive encouragement and support from my friends and family. I learned what matters most in life is not money, fame, and recognition. What matters most is the relationships we build and the hearts we touch.

Along the way to the top position of National Marketing Director, when fear rose up in me, and when doubt reared itself and told me that I would never make it to the top, I stopped those thoughts and inner voices. I replaced them with a powerful visualization of my daughters and me standing on the main stage at the Memphis Conference. This visualization led to action. I made more calls, scheduled and hosted more events, and supported my developing leaders. I focused on a photograph of my children until I cried. They were my reason for working so hard, for developing myself, for advancing my business.

In October 2007 my family joined me in Memphis to celebrate my promotion to National Marketing Director. I was scheduled to speak to over 5,000 people who had gathered from all around the world for the Juice Plus+ conference. I had memorized my speech and practiced at least 100 times in front of the mirror, my daughters, and team partners. Our family gathered backstage one hour prior to my giving the speech. This was the first time I had spoken or stepped foot in front of a large corporate audience, the first time to walk across a stage flooded with lights, the first time to speak to thousands of people.

Elegant foods and beverages were provided in a room back stage for all the new National Marketing Directors . Outside our comfort zone, my daughters and I held hands and remained silent. The backstage crew, corporate leaders, and staff tended to their obligations. Some of the important leaders I knew from other conferences, calls, and my years of involvement walked by. I felt out of place. I was not the only one. Some of the other new leaders scheduled to go on stage were nervous. I took in a few deep breaths to prepare.

I was the first scheduled speaker. All eyes turned on my family and me. A crewman directed us to line up by the stairs leading to the stage. I felt faint and light-headed. Fear flooded my being. My mouth was dry. I felt inadequate. *What if you trip? What if you talk too fast? What if you forget your speech?* I quieted those thoughts with positive affirmations, shifted my fear to faith, and reminded myself why I was giving the speech—to inspire others. "God, calm my heart, allow my words to touch at least one heart," I prayed.

"Ten seconds to go," the crewman informed us. My thoughts slowed down, and I felt God take over. My daughters, lined up behind me, were the reason I committed to this goal. I made the commitment to set an example and inspire them. God's gift, they helped me through Dave's illness and the fears and grief that came with his passing. They beamed at me with pride. I felt Dave's calming presence. The most important people in my life were my family. The most important job was being a great mother. My daughters were my trophy. They were my promotion. They were my heroes. Their love, belief, and support enabled me to develop into a leader and serve more people.

An announcer called my name. I walked onto the stage followed by Stephanie, Sarah, Megan, and Michelle. As I walked, the song I had selected for this occasion, *You Raise Me*

Up, by Josh Groban, played. The song portrayed the way I felt—humbled, grateful, and excited. I received the National Marketing Director plaque and held it up. Then I handed it to Stephanie to hold while I gave my speech. I introduced my daughters, lined up to the left of me in birth order. I shared the story of how raw food, Juice Plus+, faith in a living God, and mighty miracles extended Dave's life for eight extra years. "This business is a personal growth course cleverly designed as a business. I am grateful to be aligned with a company full of integrity. I love this business culture and community," I shared. Towards the conclusion of my speech, I spotted a mentor who had helped me throughout the entire journey. She stood in front of the stage with her hands over her heart, tears streaming down her face, mouthing the words, "Look where you can go. I believe in you."

After my speech, I received a standing ovation. I felt profound gratitude and fulfillment. I walked off the stage. A professional photographer and friends snapped pictures. Colleagues and mentors showered me with love, bouquets of flowers, and congratulations. Sarah waited for the crowd to disperse and approached me. She opened her arms and offered a warm and full embrace, one I will never forget. "When I grow up," she whispered, "I want to be just like *you*."

Time stood still. I held onto Sarah. I saw nothing else. I heard nothing. This moment was for us. Sarah, in sharing her heartfelt authentic feelings when Dave passed, helped me realize that I needed to fill my own shoes. In so doing, I was now inspiring her to fill her own.

34
Unwanted Truth

There are no coincidences in the Universe,
only convergences of Will, Intent, and Experience.
Neale Donald Walsch

Sarah

Almost a year after Dad's passing, the telephone rang in the kitchen one afternoon.

"Hello," I answered.

No response.

"Hello," I repeated. "Is anyone there?"

Silence.

I hung up and told Mom that the phone needed to be fixed. She picked up the phone. "It's not broken," she said. I took the receiver, placed it over my right ear, and then my left ear. I could only hear the dial tone with my left ear. I figured water from the shower had filled my right ear. I tapped my head, trying to get the water out. That didn't change anything. I slept on my right ear, hoping that would help. No success. After a week of those efforts, I still couldn't hear out of my right ear.

175

Mom set up an appointment with a local ear doctor who conducted a hearing test. He informed us that I was deaf in my right ear, most likely due to a virus. In an effort to try and regain some hearing, he prescribed a steroid, though it was unlikely my hearing would be restored. I took the medication for two months. The side effects were horrible—bone pain, weight gain, and a swollen face, devastating to me.

Distraught by the side effects, I was even more distressed by the fact that my hearing had still not returned. I had a hard time hearing basic conversations and grew self-conscious at large gatherings. I blushed when I asked people to repeat what they had said, or when I responded to half-understood questions. I felt frustrated when eating at a noisy restaurant with friends. I learned to sit at the particular end of the table that would allow me to avoid turning my head and straining my neck in order to hear. Since I no longer discerned the direction of sound, when someone called my name in a crowd, I looked in front of me, to my right, to my left, and behind me, in an effort to locate the person calling my name. The process was embarrassing, as was losing my equilibrium. I began to lose my balance.

I became overwhelmed with my new life. Dad was gone and so was my hearing. Once again, I fell into a depression and isolated myself from others. I distanced myself from my friends at school and began spending more time by myself. I went for long walks along the golf cart paths, searching for understanding in nature. I began journaling to express my feelings, to receive insight, and to acquire new understandings. I also searched the Scriptures for answers to the many questions of my heart. As my relationship with the Lord grew stronger, I began hoping and praying that my hearing would be restored.

Seven and a half years later, I graduated with a bachelor's degree in education from Brigham Young University in Rexburg, Idaho. I was offered several choices for student teaching and after praying, I decided to move to Arizona. Having never lived there, I was excited for the new experience. I envisioned myself teaching high school students and inspiring them to make good choices and find meaning in their lives. I imagined myself finding the love of my life and starting a family. I wondered about where I would live after student teaching ended. In which district would I work? How would my classroom look?

One weekend in mid-October, while student teaching at Mesa High School, I was invited over to my Uncle Steve's house, Dad's oldest brother. He was curious about how I liked teaching, and how I was getting along with my new roommates. He proceeded to tell me about a hearing device for individuals who suffered from single-sided deafness.

Uncle Steve worked with a man named Ross, who he observed pick up the telephone one afternoon. The man tried listening from his deaf ear and burst into laughter. He had forgotten to put in his SoundBite hearing device. He explained to my uncle that he was deaf in one of his ears and needed the device to hear. The bones, he elaborated, are conductors for sound. The hearing device consisted of a small retainer placed on the top molar on the side of his good ear and a hearing aid on his deaf ear. The sound was re-routed through his teeth and jawbone to the cochlea, bypassing the middle and outer ear, and restoring hearing in the impaired ear.

Amazed, my uncle wondered if the device could work for me. He encouraged me to check out the recent invention, only offered by a few physicians, one of whom practiced in Phoenix, Arizona.

The following Monday morning, I called the doctor's office to set up an appointment. Due to a cancelation, the doctor had time to see me the next day. Eager to learn more about the recent invention, I checked my schedule and penciled in the appointment: Tuesday at 4:00 p.m.

The next day after the school bell rang, I gathered my belongings, walked to my car, and drove to the city. I arrived and checked in the doctor's office at the appointed time. As I met with the doctor, he asked me several questions and took notes. First, he wanted to know when the hearing loss began.

"I was seventeen. My ear doctor back home told me my hearing loss was caused by a virus," I explained.

"A virus!"

"Yes, the doctor said that sometimes a virus can get in the cell of the inner ear and cause deafness."

"Did you ever get an MRI?"

"No."

He appeared shocked. "You should have an MRI done immediately to rule out the possibility of a tumor," he added.

"A tumor," I exclaimed with a laugh. "Don't you think if I had a tumor in my head for eight years that I would know by now?"

He remained quiet for a moment, pondering. "You do appear to be in fairly good physical health. Judging from that, I would say no. But we still need to make sure."

I felt rather annoyed with his persistence over scheduling an MRI. Tumors? Not me. That just wasn't possible. And what about this hearing device? Why should I pay a lot of money for something that might not work?

"Do you have a hearing device I might try?" I asked.

"Yes, the doctor said." After setting me up with the hearing device, I was overjoyed that the apparatus worked. For the first time in eight years, I could hear out of both ears. There was no delayed or robotic sound. Eager to have my own SoundBite, I was ready to pay cash, right then and there.

The doctor insisted that I get an MRI before proceeding. He ordered the test for the following week. I considered the appointment a major inconvenience but complied. Soon, I would hear out of both ears again! Soon, I would have this wonderful technology in my possession!

A month prior, I began applying for permanent teaching positions and had several possibilities lined up. During this period of time, I felt a strong sense of urgency to complete my student teaching observations and portfolio binder. I was not a procrastinator, but this sense of urgency was keener than usual. As a result, I completed the finishing touches the day before my twenty-fifth birthday, earlier than required.

Life was at an all-time high on November 3, 2013. I celebrated my birthday at my Uncle Steve's house surrounded by my aunt, cousins, and friends. I had just completed my student teaching requirements and felt blessed, accomplished, and ready to create a bright future in education. As I blew out the candles on my birthday cake, I closed my eyes and visualized my dreams coming true in the upcoming year.

35
Screeching Halt

The sun rises each morning and sheds light on things we might have overlooked the days or years before.
Tyler Hebert

Sarah

After school the next day, I drove to the Doctor's office for a follow-up appointment. I couldn't stop smiling. I felt blessed. This recent invention would change my life. I had already talked to Mom, equally as excited. She promised to give me the hearing device for Christmas, several weeks away.

As I checked in, the receptionist handed me an MRI report. I sat down in the waiting room and scanned the papers. My eyes latched onto the words, "large enhancing mass on the right posterior part of the brain." Obviously, the receptionist had mistaken me for someone else. But there was my name. Sarah Smartt. I touched my right ear, the ear that had heard with the help of the hearing device. A large mass? In my brain? I moved my hand down the side of my head. This couldn't be.

The doctor opened the door to the waiting room. "Sarah Smartt," he called, sounding serious and sober.

I followed him down a hallway to his office. "You have a tumor, and it's big," he said, with such directness that I was taken aback.

Even though I had read the words on the report, I couldn't believe it. I couldn't have a tumor. I couldn't have cancer. I sat down and placed a hand over my mouth. I felt faint. Everything around me became a blur.

The doctor proceeded to show me the MRI. He traced the image of my brain and pointed to the tumor, zooming in on the image. He seemed fascinated by the size of the mass.

A brain tumor? I hadn't even considered the possibility, even though I had struggled with health challenges and some odd symptoms. Throughout the years, I suffered from severe migraines. Since one of the causes of headaches is dehydration, I began drinking so much water that some of my friends teased me, saying I drank water like a camel. Imbalance and dizziness bothered me as well. Once I fainted for no reason. I brushed it off. I assumed that I needed to rest because of overextending myself. Then I began experiencing weakness in my legs when I jogged. The most aggravating of all was constipation.

I knew something was wrong, but when I went to the doctors for answers, they ordered a few tests and reported that the results were normal. I had wondered if the doctors thought the symptoms were all in my head. Now I knew the symptoms were not psychosomatic; they were the result of a brain tumor. My initial hearing loss was a result of the tumor blocking my hearing canal. How had I become the victim to such a misdiagnosis?

"Am I going to die?" I managed to say, breaking down and sobbing.

"If you don't get surgery to remove the tumor, then yes, you will die."

Where was the empathy? What kind of misguided consolation was this? I was furious, even more so when toward the end of the visit, he finally shared a crucial detail - that the tumor was not cancerous.

Before leaving, the doctor led me to his receptionist. She set up an appointment for me to talk with a neurosurgeon. Enraged by the doctor's lack of bedside manners, I stormed out of the office and sat in my car. I regretted going to the appointment. I didn't want a diagnosis. I didn't want a tumor. I wanted to remain in oblivion. My entire body shook with fear. I replayed the moment the doctor's finger traced the mass on my brain. I shuddered. How could I return to my apartment and face my roommates? When would I have the surgery? How could I break the news to Mom?

Finally I rallied up the courage and picked up my phone. After hearing Mom's voice on the other line, I burst into tears.

Rachel

Sarah sobbed and managed to inform me that she had a massive brain tumor. My knees buckled and I collapsed onto a chair. I felt hot and dizzy. My heart sank. How could this be? Sarah? A brain tumor? I pictured her all alone in her apartment trying to comprehend this devastating news. I wanted to be there to provide comfort.

But then my thoughts switched from imagining Sarah to picturing Dave. "Please, God, not again. Don't allow this to happen to our family a second time. Sarah's too young. She has dreams and a passion to teach. Don't take that from her."

Then anger rose up in me. How could all the doctors have missed this? Why had they not order an MRI when she lost her hearing? Why had I not insisted on one?

We sobbed, fell into a temporary silence, cried some more, and struggled to comprehend. I knew there was a purpose for everything in life. Helping Dave for so many years enabled me to overcome fear and grow in my faith. I had learned to trust in and rely on the Lord. I believed there were no accidents, no mistakes. Everything was in God's hands. All challenges and tragedies were opportunities to draw closer to Him and to serve others.

I realized God's hand in this situation. Sarah could have been in another state doing her student teaching, but she was in Arizona. Because she was in Arizona, she spent time with my brother-in-law, who had recommended the hearing device that was previously unknown to us. The doctor who could order the hearing device had insisted upon an MRI. If he had not, we might not have known about the tumor. And then, Sarah had finished her teaching portfolio ahead of time.

I shared these details with Sarah to give her hope. We didn't believe in coincidence. We trusted Heavenly Father was present. Our God was a loving God. "Sarah, if there's anyone who can rise to the occasion with strong faith, I know it's you. You have been through hard times before. You have felt the Spirit of the Lord. You know the power of prayer. The bigger the tumor, the bigger God can show up like He always has done," I said.

Sarah

Mom booked the earliest flight and flew to Phoenix. Uncle Steve picked her up from the airport and drove her to my apartment. I burst into tears as we embraced. She comforted and assured me that all would be okay, but would it?

Later that afternoon, Uncle Steve drove Mom and me to meet with a top neurosurgeon at Barrow Neurological Institute, world-renowned for brain research and surgery. We were escorted to an examining room. Mom and Uncle Steve sat in the chairs next to mine. Trying to remain calm, we made small talk while waiting for the doctor. Dr. Randall Porter knocked on and opened the door, introducing himself. His tone was serious. He shook my hand and turned on the computer to show the MRI scan to us. As I looked at the scan, my stomach turned into knots. Mom sat there, wide-eyed and speechless. Dr. Porter diagnosed the tumor as an acoustic neuroma. "This is by far the largest tumor I have ever seen," he explained. "It's putting tremendous pressure on your brain." He was shocked by my general sense of well-being considering the size of the tumor.

About six centimeters, comparable to the size of a plum, the mass was considered gigantic. Though noncancerous, the tumor had displaced my brain stem over three centimeters. Its asymmetrical shape complicated matters. "This is more serious than a stage four brain tumor," he said, "and extremely rare for someone so young. The tumor is sitting on the most important part of the body. This is urgent. You need to have surgery as soon as possible."

The surgery to remove the tumor was as complicated, if not more so, than open heart surgery. The surgery would take place over three days. The first day would involve twelve hours in the operating room. Dr. Porter would shave the side of my head, make a big incision, and begin the lengthy procedure of removing the mass. The tumor was squeezing the top of my brain. When they removed the tumor, the brain would be able to relax and move back in place, which the doctor explained, was a slow process and would require all of the second day. The third day would demand an additional ten hours for the doctor to go back in and remove the remainder of the tumor.

Those factual details bothered me less than learning about the potential complications following surgery. The doctor saw it as his professional duty to inform me of the possible outcomes. His list was devastating: stroke, coma, brain damage, raspy voice, speech problems, blurred vision, breathing difficulties requiring a tracheostomy, inability to swallow requiring a feeding tube, and severe balance issues requiring a walker or wheelchair.

"The tumor has been stretching out your right facial muscle for so long, and, as a result, your face will droop after its removal," he added.

I placed my right hand on my right cheek. My face would droop? How could this be?

"There is also no possibility that your hearing will return," he continued. "I'm very sorry to have to tell you this news. I wish your case was different."

"Just pull the plug," I responded, looking the doctor straight in the eyes. I sat there barely able to breathe. I wanted a different life. How could I possibly serve as a teacher with all of these complications? How would I ever get married and raise a family of my own?

That night I cried myself to sleep. I felt trapped in a nightmare from which I couldn't wake. I wanted to run from the surgery scheduled five weeks away on December 17th, but there was nowhere to go. My icy fear of the unknown overtook me. I was in complete despair and felt abandoned by God.

36
Necessary Steps

Only God can turn a mess into a message, a test into a testimony,
A trial into triumph, a victim into a victory.
Unknown

Sarah

The following morning I woke with a throbbing headache. I had no more tears left to cry. I took some Advil and got dressed. Mom suggested we drive to the Temple and take time to contemplate in a quiet and peaceful place. On the drive there, I remembered a quote from the modern apostle Elder Robert D. Hales: "When you want to speak to God, pray. And when you want Him to speak to you, search the Scriptures."

We sat down in the chapel, held hands, and bowed our heads. Mom whispered, "Oh Father, we are grateful for your protection over Sarah. Thank you for her overall good health throughout the years. We recognize your hand in discovering this unexpected tumor. We are scared. We desperately need Your Guidance and the peace of surrendering to Your Will." Mom's words were powerful and helped to lift my heart.

I then picked up a Bible and opened to Psalms 70-71, the words of David asking God to remember him, words I felt deeply and could not express.

"Make haste, O God, to deliver me; make haste to help me, Oh Lord. Deliver me... for thou art my hope and trust from my youth... thou art my help and my deliverer; Oh Lord, make no tarrying... be not far from me, make haste for my help... and let such as love thy salvation say continually, Let God be magnified."

Let God be magnified were the words that penetrated my heart. Because of the miracles I had witnessed throughout my life, my confidence and faith were strong. I was only eight years old when Dad was diagnosed with terminal cancer. Initially, the doctors gave him six months to live, but his life was extended for eight years. This life extension allowed me the blessing of having my father present during the critical stage of adolescence. Dad was a man full of integrity and a true giver. He gave me life, and he taught me how to live life. I treasure the memories that extra time allowed us to create; I will especially cherish our late night discussions about the Creation and the ministry of Jesus Christ.

When I turned twenty-one, I decided to serve an eighteen-month mission for my church. Every day for a year and a half, I preached the Gospel of Jesus Christ. I witnessed divine intervention and healing for individuals who prayed with faith. Some of the most complicated situations were made right. Addicts were given the power to overcome their addictions. One elderly woman fasted and prayed that the pain from her arthritis would lessen. The next day we went to her house to check up on her. God had heard her prayer, she testified. She was pain-free.

Numerous individuals took the necessary steps to come closer to Jesus Christ and enter the waters of baptism. One man received a surprise raise after tithing. Rather than living in fear, his old way of being, he trusted God would provide. Disunity and bitter feelings plagued another family. After accepting the truth we shared with them, they practiced genuine forgiveness and made the decision to start anew. The spiritual and physical changes I observed on my mission were nothing short of miraculous. Individuals and families were transformed. The light in their eyes brightened.

After returning from my mission, I enrolled at Brigham Young University in Idaho. I felt that God was guiding me to change my major from business to Spanish education. When I checked out the requirements for a Spanish education major, I was overwhelmed. Why so many literature requirements? How would I ever read full books in Spanish? Automotive engineering seemed less daunting, and I had no interest or talent in engineering. Anything else, please. But, no matter how much I pleaded and bargained, I felt pulled to change my major to Spanish education. I sensed that was God's will for me, and I decided to obey.

I walked to the academic advising center and changed my major. I accessed the Lord's power through prayer and relied upon His strength from that moment on, semester after semester. If God could part the Red Sea and move mountains, then surely He could help me pass my classes. God carried me every step of the way through my graduation in Spring 2013. I received a bachelor's degree in Spanish education. As I walked to the graduation ceremony, wearing cap and gown, I looked to the sky. The Spirit penetrated my entire being, and I had full conviction that God lived.

God had proven Himself in the past, so why not now? Why wouldn't God come through when I so desperately needed Him? I realized that the common denominator with each miracle was not just praying, but praying with faith. Throughout my life, the Lord had been tutoring me about faith and how to trust in Him. Now was the time to let Him be magnified.

I knew that miracles occur when one is tried in his or her faith. I needed to completely surrender. I needed to have full faith in God. I made the decision right then and there to stop complaining and start believing in a positive outcome. Our God was All-Powerful. Our God could perform miracles.

The very next day my student teaching supervisor called to inform me that I was granted an early release from student teaching, and that I would receive full credit because all of my requirements were completed earlier in the semester. I also learned that a major financial concern was no longer a problem. I feared that I might have to pay for the million-dollar surgery out of pocket, if Mom's insurance no longer covered dependents my age. Thankfully, we learned that dependents were covered up to the age of twenty-six. I was twenty-five. The timing was impeccable. I praised God for the tender mercy.

During the critical weeks ahead, instead of crying myself to sleep at night, I began studying the Scriptures. I read and pondered on how Jesus cleansed the leper, raised Lazarus from the dead, and fed a multitude of five thousand with only five loaves of bread and two fish. When He gave sight to the man who was born blind, Jesus explained that the reason for the man's disability was "for the glory of God to be manifested."

The miracles that Jesus performed were not reserved for those special few in history - those he ministered to when He walked upon the earth. They were available to everyone, including me. The Lord desired to heal me. I could feel that in my heart. "All things are possible to him that believeth" (Mark 9:23). My brain tumor was not bigger than God. There was no limit to God's power. Throughout history, God had defied the laws of nature. Medical doctors could diagnose and give a predicted outcome, but in the end the Lord had the final say. My

Resurrected Savior was the Master Physician and the Ultimate Healer.

I realized I was the defining variable. If I chose to partner with Him, He could change my fate. I made the decision in that moment to completely depend upon my Savior. I sensed His eagerness to fight the battle that lay ahead of me. I felt similar to David before he defeated Goliath.

The night before the surgery, adrenalin flowed. I didn't sleep much. The alarm buzzed at four a.m., and Mom and I drove to the hospital in the dark. I focused on the Lord's ability to perform the impossible. "Let God be magnified. Let God be magnified," I repeated over and over in my mind. Confident in God's power, I surrendered my life and my future into His hands.

When I entered the hospital, my surgeon asked if he could pray with me. There was no hesitation on my part. I was happy and grateful that he asked. He bowed his head and proceeded to ask the Lord for protection over my body and to assist him during the next few days of surgery.

After signing a few final consent forms, I excused myself to the restroom to change into a hospital gown. I looked at myself in the mirror, took a deep breath, and kneeled down on the cold tile. There, I prayed with all of my heart and soul. "Heavenly Father, now is the time to show who you are. Encircle me in the arms of your protection, so I can walk away without any complications. Help the surgeon and other medical professionals feel your presence today. Sharpen their minds and guide their hands. I believe you can heal my body and make me whole again. You can do anything! Let's blow everyone away with your power today, okay? I still have work to accomplish on this earth. I want to live free of disabilities! I want to serve mankind and tell the world of your greatness, but I need your help. By myself I am weak, but with you, I am strong."

Before entering the operating room, I hugged Mom. I lay down on the stretcher, and the anesthesiologist injected the syringe. "Oh God, this is it! Both hands are up. It's your time to shine," I thought, and then the room went dark.

37
Waiting

Faith isn't faith until you surrender.
Unknown

Rachel

As I watched Sarah wheeled off to the operating room for surgery, my heart sank. If only I could trade places with her. If only I could prevent the pain that follows such a massive surgery. I took in a deep breath and followed the directions of a receptionist who pointed me toward a locker room where I could store my belongings.

As I opened a random empty locker, something inside me said, "Look up." I couldn't break my gaze from the number of the locker - seven. Dave had passed away on the seventh of January. He had promised that he would never miss any of our children's big events. He wasn't going to miss the operation. I could feel him with my entire being. He wasn't going to let anything happen to our baby girl.

I returned to the waiting room and joined my brother, sister-in-law, and two close friends. We sat together, believed in the best outcome together, and prayed together. I had relied on prayer and visualization throughout my life. I believed in bringing specific requests to God. Sarah had told me before surgery that one of her biggest concerns was the possibility of having to live with a droopy face the rest of her life. She didn't want that. When I prayed, I visualized friends and family members offering devotions on Sarah's behalf. I saw the powerful effects of these prayers entering Sarah's facial muscles. I envisioned the muscles on both sides of her face remaining strong and tight. Throughout the day, I pulled the elastic of a band I wore around my wrist as a reminder to imagine Sarah with a symmetrical smile.

After thirteen long hours, the nurse reported, to our surprise, that the surgeons were done. She guided us to a private waiting room and explained that the doctor would arrive shortly. The five of us held hands. Our hearts felt like they were bursting out of our chests. We had prayed and fasted all day. We had chosen to remain positive, despite our concerns and worries. Standing there waiting, I began to tremble. What if something had gone wrong?

The doctor entered the room and sat down in front of us. "The surgery went far better than expected. I was able to remove the tumor and get as close to the brainstem as possible. There's no need for additional surgery. This is unheard of - not running into any complications and sailing right through such a massive operation."

He added that he checked Sarah's facial muscles during surgery, and they were healthy and strong. "This is the largest acoustic neuroma that I've ever seen. Most small tumors cause complete facial paralysis. The success we've experienced is rare. I feel humbled and give all credit to God."

We all bowed our heads and wept tears of relief and gratitude. I thanked Heavenly Father for guiding the surgeon's hands and the success of the surgery. I wanted to hug Dave and the angels in attendance. I knew they would continue to watch

Sarah as she recovered. Eager to see Sarah, I followed as she was wheeled into a room in the intensive care unit. Though she lay there pale and unconscious, she was glowing.

38
Christmas Miracle

Where there is hope there is faith.
Where there is faith miracles happen.
Anonymous

Sarah

I woke up in the ICU. My arms were strapped to the bed. A breathing tube was in my throat. I couldn't move. I couldn't talk. I had to know how the surgery went. I lifted my fingers up and down, pretending to write. The nurse understood my sign language. She handed me a pencil and paper. "Am I okay? How did it go?" The words were sloppy, the anesthesia and post-op drowsiness creating a drunken-like sprawl of letters.

"The surgery went better than expected," the nurse said, just as Mom walked in the room. Seeing me awake, she rushed over and offered a gentle hug.

"The surgery was miraculous," she assured. "You were only in the operating room for thirteen hours because everything went smoothly! Dr. Porter checked your facial muscles during surgery. He said that they were very healthy and strong. There's no need to worry about a droopy face."

I felt relieved and managed a smile.

A male nurse entered the room. His job was to remove the breathing tube. After he did, I gasped for air. Everyone in the room cheered. I could breathe on my own. If my lungs had collapsed, the nurse would have had to insert another breathing tube. I sighed with relief. That was one more complication I didn't have to worry about.

Twenty-four hours after surgery, a swallowing specialist entered the room to see if I could eat. The nurse raised the bed, so I could attempt to sit up for the first time. Blood rushed to my head. I felt dizzy and nauseous. I had no appetite. The eating specialist provided me a cracker and juice. I was asked to take a bite of the cracker and sip the juice through the straw. I could chew and swallow. More cheers resounded through the room. One more possible obstacle vanished. I smiled. Everyone cheered. A simple smile and a single spoken word were celebrated.

I then wished to see my scar. Mom held two small mirrors up to my head. One in the front and one in the back. "Oh my goodness," I said, wide-eyed. Half of my head was bald. The scar was larger than I had imagined. I touched my head and cringed as I slid my finger down the length of the incision, feeling each stitch. I rubbed my fingers together and snapped them together near my right ear.

"I can hear," I said to Mom.

"Really?" She walked around to my right side and whispered, "Sarah, I love you. Can you hear me?"

"I love you too," I said. My eyes filled with tears of joy.

Mom hugged me and squeezed my hand. She pondered for a moment, a questioning look in her eyes. I could almost read her mind. How could my hearing return when that was impossible, according to several doctors. "Let's call Stephanie," she said, as she hit the speedy dial for my older sister. "If you can hear her, then we'll know for sure that your hearing has returned." She placed the cell phone up to my previously deaf ear.

"Hello," my sister said.

"Hey. It's Sarah. Say something. I want to see if I can hear you."

"Uh… I love you so much, and I'm so happy to hear that you are okay!"

"Aha! I can HEAR your voice," I exclaimed, wanting to jump up and down and shout for joy!

The surgeon then walked into the room.

"Guess what?" I said, beaming with excitement.

"What?"

"I can hear out of my right ear."

"No you can't."

"Yes I can. I just talked with my sister on the phone and could hear her voice in my right ear."

The doctor walked around the bed. He rubbed his fingers near my right ear. "You can hear that?" he asked, with skepticism in his voice.

"Yep," I said, smiling.

He stepped back, placed his hand on his chin, and stared at me for a few seconds. "Well, that is scientifically impossible, because the tumor had completely destroyed your entire hearing canal and cochlear nerve," he said. He blinked, shook his head, and stood there staring at me, unable to provide a logical explanation. After moments of silence, I pointed towards heaven. He smiled and said, "I would agree."

Learning how to walk again humbled me. The third day after surgery, I stood at the end of the hall with both hands on a walker. Which foot was I supposed to put in front of the other? How could I forget something so simple? I felt weak and incapable of accomplishing even the simplest task. Discouragement set in. I tried to hold back tears, although Mom noticed that I was struggling. "You can do this, Sarah," Mom cheered me on. After a few minutes, I managed to move my right foot forward. Each step required concentration and effort. After inching my way down the hall, I called out for a wheelchair. The nurse grabbed one and helped me sit down. My whole body collapsed. I had no energy. I couldn't stand. I couldn't hold my head upright. Mom wheeled me back to the room, trying to avoid any minor bumps on the ground. "Let's get you back in bed, Honey. We're going to take things one day at a time," she said.

The following day, a nurse elevated the bed and pulled down the sheets. "Time to practice walking," she said. I didn't want to walk. Nauseous and weak, I wanted to remain in bed, but the nurse reached over to help me sit up. I let out a deep sigh. "Get up when you're ready," she encouraged me. I closed my eyes and offered a silent prayer, "Oh God, help me! I don't have the strength to walk."

"I got you through surgery. Now trust Me in your recovery," were the words I heard back.

After a moment of silence, a glimmer of hope filled me, and I lifted both hands in the air to motion that I was ready. The nurse wheeled the walker over to the bed. I managed to stand up. Mom cheered me on, as I struggled to walk from the bed to the door. Although exhausted, as if I had finished a race, a flicker of determination was ignited. Maybe I could walk without the walker. I asked Mom to help me. She stood in front of me and held out her hands. Could I do it? The nurse pulled the walker to the side. I grasped Mom's hands. "Don't let go," I said with anxiety in my voice. I hobbled down the hallway. Accomplishing more than I thought I could, I decided to try walking by myself. Mom smiled and let go of my hands. At first, I walked like a robot. Wasn't I supposed to swing my arms? Which arm for which foot? Who knew? I just kept at it, taking one step, then another.

The doctors had predicted before surgery that I would remain in the hospital several weeks to months, depending on the severity of complications. Miraculously, I walked out of the hospital five days after the surgery. We stayed in Gilbert with close friends from our church in Georgia. They had moved to Arizona, only half an hour away from the hospital. When they heard about my surgery, they opened their home to my family who flew in from around the country. They cleared out belongings from their luxurious master suite so we could rest in comfort. A seating area in the room provided extra space for our family to gather. I slept in their king-sized bed and treasured the coziness of the fireplace. Mom slept in the bed with me. Megan and Michelle slept in the kid's room. Stephanie, her husband Stephen and their two little boys stayed at Uncle Steve's house and drove over each morning to see how I was doing. Our friends and their four small children slept in a camper in their yard. I felt deep gratitude for their selfless generosity.

Most of the time we spent in Gilbert, I remained in bed. Even though I was out of the hospital and off all pain medications, I was still facing recovery from the trauma of major surgery. I was fatigued and my head still hurt, but I chose to focus on and appreciate that I could hear. I had prayed for God to restore my hearing for over eight years. Only the Lord knew this secret yearning of my heart. Just when I was beginning to consider that God was late in answering my prayers, events occurred that now astonished me. What if I had not switched my major to Spanish Education? What if I had not chosen Arizona to do my student teaching? What if I never heard about the hearing device? What if the ear doctor had not insisted that I get an MRI? What if I had not been guided to such a skilled neurosurgeon? What if I had not fully trusted in the Lord?

Overwhelmed at the order of events, I felt awe and gratitude for God's wisdom, foresight, and timing. He had been guiding my steps for years and was aware of all the details in my life. I couldn't hold back the tears. I loved God with every ounce of my heart. He was my loyal friend who never left my side. He had not abandoned me like I once thought, but rather gifted me with a miracle. How could I ever adequately thank Him for saving my life?

In the evenings, I managed to get out of bed and walk into the kitchen where everyone gathered and visited. I held onto the walls and took one careful step after another, moving slowly to steady my balance. Protective of my head, I held it in a stiff position. When I needed to turn to the left or right, I swiveled my whole body in that direction. Self-conscious of my scar, I wore my hair down to cover it.

Christmas morning, I sat propped up in bed with a pillow supporting my back. The fire crackled in the fireplace. Family members opened a few small gifts. *Silent Night, The Little Drummer Boy, O Holy Night* and other carols played in the background. I treasured the melodies I knew by heart. Joy flooded my entire being. Having my hearing restored was the most wonderful Christmas gift I had ever received.

Two weeks after the surgery, I flew home to Georgia. Numerous friends provided assistance. One charitable couple flew from Georgia to Arizona in order to drive my car back home. I received encouraging notes and loving visits. Warm meals arrived and relieved Mom from having to worry about what to prepare for dinner. The heartfelt prayers, love, and simple acts of kindness will never be forgotten.

While I was surrounded by such generosity and felt grateful for my restored hearing and the successful removal of the tumor, I was soon humbled by the reality of recovering from major brain surgery. Deep fatigue and headaches were part of my struggle in the days, months, and year ahead. Insomnia worsened these effects. I would not have been able to navigate through these challenges without the loving support of my mom. She demonstrated selflessness, kindness, empathy, and patience. Her strong courage and faith helped to ignite mine. She believed in mighty miracles and helped me believe as well. The Lord had brought my mother and me back together. He allowed us time to rely on and learn from each other. Our relationship had been mended and was now being strengthened.

One afternoon about six months after surgery, I was taking my dog for a brief walk. A neighbor down the street, about my age, had also been hospitalized for major surgery to remove a brain tumor. I happened to walk past his house as he was returning from the hospital. I watched his parents help him out of the car. The mom reached her arm around one side of her son. The dad, on the other side, steadied his balance. They attempted to move from the car to the house, but about half way there, the young man stopped, obviously too exhausted to continue walking. His dad lovingly picked him up and carried him inside. My heart went out to them. Witnessing how his dad carried him caused me to reflect on how my own mother was carrying me through this difficult time. Even more importantly, the Savior was holding and loving me more than I realized. The Lord knew exactly how I and my neighbor hurt, how we both felt overwhelmed by the emotional and physical pain. He knew how our parents were committed to our care. I knew in the depths of my being that the timing was perfectly aligned for me to witness that moment and to feel a glimmer of the love and care the Savior feels for all of us.

I continued to rest and wait for my strength and energy to return, and I prayed for patience. I learned that some miracles are instantaneous, and some are progressive. God steps in and can do the impossible with a snap of a finger, or He can run alongside us as we cover the challenging miles of a marathon. My hearing was restored in a day. Recovery from brain surgery was a different matter. This was the marathon I didn't feel up to running. I could only take one step at a time, often with a long nap to recover from the shortest of strides.

After eight long months of deep fatigue and headaches, I wondered if I would ever feel normal again. After the removal of a brain tumor, cognitive changes occurred. I was plagued with depression and anxiety that were difficult to overcome, since I had to spend most days in bed. I kept connected with friends through Facebook. Some friends with whom I had graduated had begun their teaching careers. Others were engaged or getting married. I was happy for my friends, but I wondered, would that ever be me? My heart ached. I felt left behind. Some nights I cried myself to sleep.

On the outside, I appeared healthier and what one might consider normal. Well-meaning friends figured that since I looked okay, I must be fully recovered. They reached out and asked, "Now what?" I hated that question. The question overwhelmed, pressured, and didn't serve me. I didn't know the answer. I still felt exhausted most of the time. I continued to suffer from severe headaches. I wasn't ready to move on with my life. I didn't need questions. I didn't need advice. I needed love. The Lord's love carried me through those difficult days.

Four months later, the post-surgical effects began to fade. Finally, I reached the one-year anniversary of the surgery and met with a doctor for the required follow-up appointment. I learned the test results of the most recent MRI were clear, indicating no tumor growth. Overjoyed, I stopped at the Jackson Street Bridge on my way home. I ripped off the medical bracelet, and I looked into the city skyline with outstretched arms. I was free. I felt better than before surgery. Even though I struggled, and would continue to struggle, with fatigue, my balance returned. My memory was improving. Headaches were an ailment of the past. My hair had grown back. I was smiling without a droopy face. I could hear again. For the first time in years, I felt whole.

More importantly, I had a new perspective and appreciation for the simple moments and joys in life. My future once again looked bright. My heart was reborn. My compassion for others increased, and my relationship with the Savior deepened. The Lord was teaching me that the greatest miracles are intangible. Although restored hearing is amazing, restored hope is more miraculous.

39
Free Falling

Only when we are no longer afraid do we begin to live.
Dorothy Thompson

Rachel

The summer of 2013 I drove to Sky Dive Georgia to find out what it would feel like to *really* fly. After watching a brief instructional video, I signed legal papers and met my assigned tandem partner. Hans, a master diver with 1000 jumps and no accidents, led me over to the hanger, where we slipped into jumpsuits to protect our clothes. As Hans strapped on my harness and protective gear, he answered numerous questions and earned my full trust. Then he attached our parachute, handed me diving goggles and high-fived me. We climbed into an empty cargo plane crammed with ten other people. Four cameramen sat in the front row taking pictures. I sat upright on the floor along with several other skydivers and our tandem instructors.

The pilot started up the engine. Soon, we ascended into the blue sky. The higher we flew, the wider my eyes. I didn't blink. I barely breathed. Hans connected himself to my harness and adjusted his goggles. Others followed suit with their instructors. We chatted about our expectations. Some were nervous about getting nauseated or passing out. The more experienced divers suggested to us beginners that we not worry because we would feel exhilarated. The master divers, our tandem instructors, echoed those sentiments and suggested that this would be the greatest and most unforgettable experience of our lives.

When we reached 12,000 feet, one of the divers opened the hatch door. The wind speed exceeded 100 miles per hour and whipped through the plane. The sound was deafening. Our gaze went to the spacious blue skies. I watched a few divers exit the plane. I shuddered. Had I really chosen to terrorize myself? Could I really do this? Jump out of this plane in less than a minute? There was no turning back. I determined to enjoy and capture every moment of the free fall. Grateful for the trusting connection between Hans and me, I took in several deep breaths.

When given direction to proceed, I shimmied to the open hatch and dangled my feet out of the plane with Hans sliding behind me. This was no easy accomplishment, since we were practically sewn together. The camera crewman shouted out to dive headfirst and then somersault in the air. And so I did. I dove as if diving into a pool. Hans followed. I couldn't tell which direction I was free falling. Was I heads up or down? Sky surrounded me on every side. Hans flipped us upright. I zoomed right through some nausea. Was I even in my body? I felt free. I felt safe. I felt like I did as a child, when I rode Penny and imagined that I was flying. Even with falling 130 miles per hour, euphoria filled me. The cool wind whipped through my hair, and vibrated my cheeks and arms. I stretched out my arms as if they were wings. I was flying.

The 7,000-foot free fall lasted for sixty seconds—a single minute that felt like three or four times as long. Hans checked in by squeezing my hands, since we couldn't see or hear each other to communicate. I gestured back with a squeeze. When it was time, Hans signaled to me that he was about to pull the parachute ripcord. I felt the upward pull. A jolt followed. Then we slowed down from 130 to twenty miles per hour in less than a few seconds. The rushing of the wind stopped. We parachuted down in absolute silence. Tranquility and serenity blanketed us.

I took in a deep breath. I noticed what was not detectable when we dove out of the plane and flew at an electrifying pace. Specks of green grass and small structures dotted the earth below. Two birds flew by the parachute. Viewing the world from the same height as birds in flight was spectacular.

Hans asked if I would like to take control of the direction of the parachute. I absolutely did. I wanted the experience to last. I wanted to focus on and see the earth and sky from many different angles. I turned the parachute to the left and then to the right. Miles of endless crystal clear sky stretched and merged with the rolling hills shadowing the horizon. The tranquility soothed my soul and slowed my beating heart. Trees, green pastures, and housetops came into view. The white fluffy clouds grew smaller as we neared the ground.

We glided for about ten minutes, the air growing warmer as we descended. We spotted the drop zone where employees of the skydiving school and spectators waved, cheered, and photographed the landing. We landed where we had started. We were home. The only part of my body that hurt was my cheeks – from smiling the entire time.

Fifteen years prior to these memorable moments, I had received the tragic news that shook my deepest being. When the doctors uttered the words "cancer" and "terminal," I felt the same shock and dread that flooded my being as I looked out into empty space, the space I would jump and free fall into at electrifying speeds. Was I falling from a fairy tale marriage into a tragedy? Dave had taken care of everything the children and I needed. Up until that moment in the doctor's office, I felt like a princess riding a stallion, the wind blowing through my hair, the sun shimmering as it lit up the sky. I enjoyed our idyllic life and had few concerns. Then we fell into a terminal diagnosis that didn't make sense to us. Were it not for pulling and holding on to the cord of my faith and belief in Jesus, I can't imagine how we would have survived. Many times after the diagnosis, I felt like I was going to crash land. Cancer forced us to slow down and pause. A stunning silence descended upon us. We paused, prayed, and reflected on God's Word. Doing so allowed us to see various perspectives of our challenges with a new set of eyes, often shifting from seeing the trial as calamity to the trial as providential, a gift to empower us. As we drifted in this motionless quiet, God touched our hearts, healed our brokenness and provided comfort. We surrendered our wills and allowed God to mold us into who He had always intended for us to be. He wanted us pliable, mirroring Him and mastering ourselves. Viewing our challenges from an eternal and higher perspective, praying with more intent, and seeking spiritual guidance, we made better choices and chose to serve through the most difficult of times.

When I ponder the eight years Dave struggled with cancer before passing on, I understand better the words of Victor Frankl, "Suffering ceases to be suffering ... in the moment that it finds meaning." Dave's life was a gift to everyone he knew — our parents, siblings, relatives, and friends. Throughout this life-changing journey, we witnessed how the Lord showed up daily and worked in our lives. God healed our wounded hearts. He gave meaning to what might be perceived as suffering and what we came to see as vital to our spiritual growth. Our daughters drew nearer to God and learned to completely trust in and surrender their lives to Him. These insights served us through Sarah's diagnosis, surgery, and recovery. We witnessed the Lord heal a physical ailment, alleviate emotional anguish, and mend a broken relationship. The strength Sarah and I acquired by relying on the Savior, Jesus Christ, through our difficulties enabled us to embrace life's possibilities and empower others in their time of need. While we had initially perceived our world as falling apart, the Lord led us to see our existence as coming into perfect alignment.

Scriptures

Blessed art thou for what thou has done; for thou has inquired of me, and behold, as often as thou has inquired thou has received instruction of my spirit. If it had not been so, thou wouldn't not have come to the place where thou art at this time. Behold, thou knowest that thou has inquired of me and I did enlighten thy mind; and now I tell thee these things that thou mayest know that thou has been enlightened by the spirit of truth.[1]
Doctrine and Covenants 6:14

Treasure up these words in thy heart. Be faithful and diligent in keeping the commandments of God, and I will encircle thee in the arms of my love. If you desire a further witness, cast your mind upon the night that you cried unto me in your heart that you might know concerning the truth of these things. Did I not speak peace to your mind concerning the matter? What great witness can you have than from God?[2]
Doctrine and Covenants 6: 20, 22, 23

And though the Lord gives you the bread of adversity, and the water of affliction, yet shall not thy teachers be removed into a corner anymore, but thine eyes shall see thy teachers.[3]
Isaiah 30:20

Fear not little flock do good... Look unto me in every thought; doubt not, fear not. . . doubt not, for it is the gift of God; and you shall hold it in your hands and do marvelous works; and no power shall be able to take it away out of your hands, for it IS the work of God.[4]
Doctrine and Covenants 6:36

There will I be also, for I will go before your face. I will be on your right hand and on your left, and my spirit shall be in your hearts, and mine angels round about to bear you up.[5]
Doctrine and Covenants 84:88

And now, my sons, remember, remember that it is upon the rock of our Redeemer, who is Christ, the Son of God, that ye must build your foundation; that when the devil shall send forth his mighty winds, yea, his shafts in the whirlwind, yea, when all his hail and his mighty storm shall beat upon you, it shall have no power over you to drag you down to the gulf of misery and endless woe, because of the rock upon which ye are built, which is a sure foundation, a foundation whereon if men build they cannot fall.[6]
Helaman 5:12

But the Lord said unto Samuel, Look not on his countenance, or on the height of his stature; for the Lord seeth not as man seeth; for man looketh on the outward appearance, but the Lord looketh on the heart.[7]
1 Samuel 16:7

* * *

About the Authors

Rachel Smartt, a Naturopathic Doctor and Nutritional Counselor, resides in Peachtree City, Georgia. She lectures nationally and trains locally on the power of whole food nutrition, staying positive in a negative world, and living authentically.

Rachel is on a mission to inspire healthy living around the world through her work as a top leader with the Juice Plus+ Company. A Lean Corporate Wellness Coach with the Sears Wellness Institute, she is passionate about prevention and anti-aging. A certified Dream Coach with Dream University, she enjoys helping her clients remove limiting beliefs, turning obstacles into opportunities, and discovering their passions.

Rachel is devoted to family and loves spending time with her four grown daughters, their husbands, and her grandchildren.

Sarah Smartt graduated from Brigham Young University - Idaho with a dual degree in Spanish Education and ESL Education. Currently, she teaches English as a Second Language at a High School in Phoenix, Arizona. Alongside her teaching, Sarah enjoys volunteering at Make-A-Wish Foundation and helping children with life-threatening medical conditions realize their dreams. In her free time, she enjoys hiking, cooking new recipes, and promoting healthy living alongside her mother.

We want to thank you, our readers, by offering a free gift.
Please visit our website:

Smarttmoderndaymiracles.com
and download 6 Solutions for Dealing with Sorrow, Suffering, and Setbacks—
a personalized meditation mp3.

1983 - The year I met Dave. He was the head pitcher for the University of Utah.

1984 - Our wedding announcement in the local newspaper.

November 1, 1984 - Our wedding day.

June 8, 1997 - This photo was taken one month following Dave's diagnosis while visiting family in Utah.

1997 - Our Family.

One of Dave's dreams was
to baptize Michelle when
she was 8 years old.

1997 - Celebrating
Dave's birthday.

June 14, 1999 - A captured moment
of Michelle (age 4) patiently waiting
to go outside and play, while Dave
finished working in his home office.

1997 - Family Portrait, the year Dave
was diagnosed with terminal cancer.

October 2005 - Three months prior
to Dave's passing.

A Beautiful message,
found 1 week after
Dave's passing.

2014 - Sky Diving Free Fall.

October 2006 - Juice Plus
Convention - Giving my
NMD Speech with the
support of my lovely
daughters Stephanie,
Sarah, Megan & Michelle.

July 2015 - Megan, Sarah,
Rachel, Stephanie, and
Michelle.

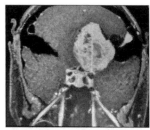

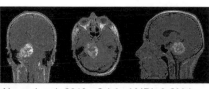

November 4, 2013 - Original MRI- 6 CM Acoustic Neuroma brain tumor.

December 18, 2013 - Hearing the news of the successful operation after waking up from surgery.

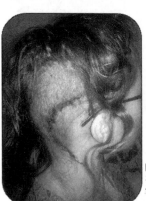

December 19, 2013 - Seeing my incision for the first time.

December 21, 2013 - Learning to walk again at BNI.

December 21, 2013 - My sisters came to my aid and supported me through those first rough days of recovery.

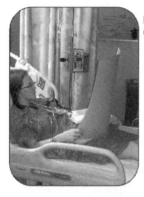

December 21, 2013 - Reading a giant Get Well card from my students.

December 25, 2013 - Christmas morning.

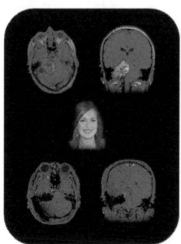

March 17, 2014 - Three months after surgery. Zero facial paralysis.

November 6, 2014 - Before and after MRI. Artwork done by Dr. Curtis Dickman.

January 7, 2015 - Celebrating my 1 Year anniversary from surgery, at the Jackson Street Bridge in Atlanta.

49884665R00133

Made in the USA
Charleston, SC
06 December 2015